Canexus:
The Canoe in
Canadian
Culture

Edited by
James Raffan & Bert Horwood
With illustrations by
Bill Mason

BETELGEUSE BOOKS

Published by Betelgeuse Books
in cooperation with Queen's University and
the Ontario Recreational Canoeing Association

Betelgeuse Books
53 Fraser Avenue
Building 7, Suite 93
Toronto, Ontario
Canada M6K 1Y7

This book is the result of a conference that was held at Queen's University Faculty of Education in the fall of 1987. Colleagues Fred Johnston, William Peruniak, Bert Horwood, and James Raffan organized a gathering and celebration called *Canexus: The Canoe in Canadian Culture*, 20-22 November, 1987, at which these authors made presentations. Our thanks to the many people at the conference—delegates, contributors, and helpers—and those who helped out afterwards—computer tamers, copy typists, readers, and editors; especially Rose Chan and Jan Carrick —whose abundant energy resulted in the genesis of this volume.

Design: Glenna Munro

Typeset and assembled using computing facilities
and Xerox 4050 printer provided by Queen's University.

Printed and bound in Canada

Canadian Cataloguing in Publication Data

Main entry under title:
Canexus: The Canoe in Canadian Culture

Co-published by the Ontario Recreational Canoeing
Association and Queen's University.
Bibliography: p.224
Includes index.
ISBN:0-9690783-5-8

1. Canoes and canoeing - Social aspects - Canada.
I. Raffan, James. II. Horwood, R.H. III. Ontario
Recreational Canoeing Association.
IV. Queen's University (Kingston, Ont.).

VM353.C36 1988   623.8'29   C88-093930-0

To Thomas L. York
1940-1988

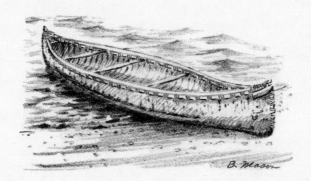

Contents

Foreword

The notion of connection that arises from the word *canexus* is a resonant structure for looking at canoe and culture. As such, I am pleased to be your guide in a preliminary exploration of the themes in this unique volume.

First, the canoe connects us to *Ma-ka-ina*, Mother Earth, from which we came and to which we must all return. Councils of those who were here before us revered the earth and also the wind, the rain, and the sun—all essential for life. It was from that remarkable blending of forces that mankind was allowed to create the canoe and its several kindred forms.

From the birch tree came the bark; from the spruce, the pliant roots; from the cedar, the ribs, planking and gunwales; and from a variety of natural sources, the sealing pitch.

In other habitats, great trees became dugout canoes while, in treeless areas, skin, bone and sinew were ingeniously fused into the kayaks. Form followed function, and manufacture was linked to available materials. Even the modern canoe, although several steps away from the first, is still a product of the earth. We have a great debt to those who experienced the land before us. No wonder that, in many parts of the world, the people thank the land for allowing its spirit to be transferred to the canoe.

Hand-propelled watercraft still allow us to pursue that elemental quest for tranquility, beauty, peace, freedom and cleanness. It is good to be conveyed quietly, gracefully, to natural rhythms.

In a very real sense the canoe connects us to Canada and to being Canadian. It reminds us of our nation's grandeur, of space—even infinity.

The canoe especially connects us to rivers—timeless pathways of the wilderness. Wave after wave of users have passed by. Gentle rains falling onto a paddler evaporate skyward to form clouds and then to descend on a fellow traveller, perhaps in another era. Likewise, our waterways contain something of the substance of our ancestors. The canoe connects us to the spirit of these people who walk beside us as we glide silently along riverine trails.

Native people also showed that the canoe connects us to other living things. For many of us who have learned to wander, the same great inspiration has become part of us. The canoe teaches us that we are part of a complex web of life and that there is interdependence between humankind and our wild neighbours—leafed, blossomed, feathered, or furred.

In a different way, the canoe connects us to those who have arrived on Canadian shores from every corner of the globe. Many immigrants have found the canoe and the beckoning wilderness to be a source of extraordinary adventure. They are excited by the treasure of open space. It is even possible that new Canadians realize the value of the natural and supernatural Canada more than long established Canadians.

And in a subtle way, the canoe connects us to a sense of security. Although some may not witness firsthand the beautiful and inspirational places, we know they exist because the canoe has shown it to be true. Those same places, in the mind's eye, came to serve as an anchor to windward in the storms and gales of life. Those places will always give generously to us the gifts of peace and solace.

The canoe connects us to alternate ways of communicating. Often without words there can be bonds formed and new understandings created, not only with other people but also with other living things. There are many messages drifting on the winds from natural places, understandings Wordsworth called "the influence of natural objects"—the quiet glory of a sunset; the excitement of migrating birds; the gentle scolding of a squirrel; the haunting call of a loon; the windsong of the wilderness.

The canoe has given rise to many beautiful images which have stimulated the creativity of those who speak through art, music, literature, dance and theatre. It connects us to these important parts of our cultural mosaic. Think of songs like "*C'est L'Aviron*" and paintings by the Group of Seven.

The canoe puts us in touch with our inner self—that still, small voice. It gives us moments of solitude in which we have the opportunity to experience, as Tennyson stated, "self-knowledge, self-reverence and self-control." In these times of insight, we are also led to things spiritual—a pause for meditation and contemplation not often experienced in the noisy, crowded, restless world.

It would be inappropriate to dwell on retrospect without at the same time reflecting on prospect. Most importantly, perhaps, the canoe connects us to our children and grandchildren who will want to paddle their craft in unobstructed, unpolluted, and unspoiled waters. As we paddle, we must be mindful of their inheritance. Let them be able to say proudly:

In the strengths of our forefathers
We have gone
Not in their footsteps
It is their stars we follow
Not their dead campfires.

This book is a cause for celebration, not only because of the canoe, but because it is created by writers who are, themselves, enthusiastic paddlers.

KIRK A.W. WIPPER
Kingston, Ontario
November 1987

Introduction

James Raffan & Bert Horwood

A portent of the canoe's place in Canadian culture is the fact that it remains the most appropriate vehicle for travelling the greater part of this boreal country. Canoes were born of the physical landscape and are ingrained in the Canadian cultural landscape. On stamps, coins, and labels, in visual art, sculpture, stained-glass windows, and advertising, canoes are omnipresent. They figure in thousands of annual trips, races, festivals, and pageants. Despite all that, the canoe as an element of Canadian culture has been uncelebrated, perhaps taken for granted. *Canexus*—first a conference held at the Queen's University Faculty of Education in November 1987, and now the book—is an effort to raise the profile of the canoe in Canadian culture, and to give it its rightful place of prominence in the consciousness of Canadians.

The word *canexus* is a neologism coined to muster images of the canoe as a connection linking people to each other, to culture, and to the land. Of primary significance, this first-of-its-kind project has served to join a disparate group of thoughtful Canadians who, until *Canexus*, had nothing in common except their love for the canoe and canoe country. As such, this collection of essays is like a beautifully complex three-dimensional reticule of images and ideas.

The book links many different ways of thinking about the canoe—ways which reflect traditional academic points of view, historical, sociological, spiritual, technological, philosophical, and ethnological perspectives. The idea behind *Canexus* was to celebrate the fundamental importance of the canoe in the development and articulation of Canadian culture.

This book is very much like the complex landscape which inspired it. There are common themes, but they do not form a coherent stream, a feature which reflects the powerful personal significance of canoes and canoeing. Yet, the odds are good that one will find, on every page, connections to other chapters or to one's own experience. This characteristic is evidence of the organic wholeness of this book: unity in diversity.

Whatever the topic, whatever the theme, a strong common element binding all chapters is the reliance upon direct and powerful personal experience. Many contributors have written personally and revealingly about critical events in their lives. Their reflections, almost meditative at times, give a freshness and authenticity to the collection. The pieces have a healthy and appealing mix of the objective and the subjective. In the whole, there is a rich synthesis of intricate interconnections and surprising insights.

Paddlers by nature are *doers*, and as a result, gatherings of paddlers tend to focus on routes and techniques. These essays break this tradition by focussing not so much on the actual, the physical, and the details; rather, attention is placed on the boats, strokes, and journeys of the imagination. Without exception, every essay in one way or another mines the mythical elements in the Canadian canoeing experience, the part of canoeing that has been transferred from the redwood and birch trees, from the lakes, and from the rivers, to the heart of consciousness.

The collection is not complete. It is doubtful if any one book on the subject could be. The voices of French Canadians and Indians have yet to be clearly heard. There is much more to be said from a feminine perspective in describing the relationship between canoe and culture. It is also important to know to what extent the canoe has influenced Canadian culture beyond the middle class, white, English population of central Canada. Is it possible that the Canadian culture for which the canoe is so powerful as a symbol is dying even as we celebrate and articulate it? Clearly, this book must be seen as but one step along a misty trail.

The only other step on this trail in recent history, is a collection of songs, poetry and prose entitled *The Romance of the Canadian Canoe,* published by Ryerson Press. In the preface, author John Murray Gibson—an Englishman by birth— wrote, "When recently I turned to see what books had been written about the Canadian Canoe, I was amazed to find how few there were, considering how much of the social history of Canada was linked up with the canoe before the building of roads and canals and railways. It seemed that something was lacking—hence this new book."

That was in 1951. As an exciting initiative in Canadian writing, *Canexus: The Canoe in Canadian Culture* bridges a 27-year gap in our literature. This is a book for paddlers, but more importantly, it is a book for non-paddlers, would-be paddlers, readers, and armchair adventurers of all kinds who have ever wondered about the canoe's place in Canadian culture.

Symbols and Myths: Images of Canoe and North

Shelagh Grant

Since the time of Confederation, Canadians have looked upon their north as a reflection of identity and destiny. Often referred to collectively as the myth of the north, various perceptions of the northern wilderness have left a lasting imprint on the national psyche, explaining the special meaning attached to the concept of north. The core myth is the least tangible: the belief that the north has imparted a unique quality to the character of the Canadian nation. At the same time, Canadians have associated various images with their concept of north that, through time, have become accepted as symbols. In contrast to the abstract ideas incorporated into myths, symbols are tangible, well defined, and visible. Although the maple leaf and the red-coated mounted policeman are perhaps the most universally acclaimed symbols of Canada, there are others which have been recognized as representing the nation's "northerness:" the beaver, the loon, the caribou and the canoe—all of which appear on our 1987 coins. The beaver and canoe, in particular, signify the centrality of the fur trade in our northern heritage.

The canoe figures prominently in other northern myths, notably the aesthetic and philosophical wilderness myths. One also could argue that the canoe represents the antithesis of the progress-oriented frontier- or nation-building myths. But what, in this context, is a myth, and what a symbol? A myth may be a traditional narrative embodying popular views of natural or social phenomena; it can be a fictitious person, thing, or idea, even a story or collection of stories. This implies that a myth is a perception rather than a fact, but a recent and convincing argument claims that fact and interpretation cannot exist independently and that myths are "attempts to depict a reality which is not easy to grasp," an inevitable result of society's efforts "to make sense of the world."[1] In essence, a myth is a perception, image or notion which explains something. The myth of the north, then, explains the impact of the north on the Canadian psyche.

Oxford defines a symbol as an object which represents or typifies an idea as a means of identification; hence the voyageur canoe is symbolic of Canada's fur trade heritage, the canvas-covered cedar strip linked with recreational sport, the kayak with the Inuit—all reflecting a close bond with the northern wilderness, past and present, but with qualification. Yet the idea of north readily conjures up other images: the midnight sun, polar bears, dog sleds, icebergs and igloos. Moreover, in relating symbols to experience, both native and non-native northerners of the Yukon and Northwest Territories tend not to perceive the canoe as symbolic of the north because of their increasing reliance on motorized boats, and because the traditional birch bark canoe was not indigenous to the region. Thus the canoe as a symbol of the north is more likely a mid-north or southern perception.

The terms "canoe" and "north" must also be clearly defined. Initially, "canoe" comes from the Caribbean Arawak language, meaning simply "a boat." However, the term became generic for deckless watercraft of the New World, whether a boat of bark or skin or a wooden dugout. By definition, "a canoe is an open watercraft of hollow form, generally shaped at each end to improve its hydrodynamic qualities, and designed originally to be propelled by one or more occupants, facing forward and using paddles or push-poles."[2] The birch bark canoe, commonly identified with the woodland Indians, and the kayak, associated with the Inuit, have been modified to accommodate current Euro-Canadian construction methods and materials, but have retained essentially the same contour lines.

In Canada, the term "north" refers not only to the politically defined Yukon and Northwest Territories, but is equally applicable to Labrador, northern Quebec and Ontario, as well as to northern regions of the prairie provinces and British Columbia. Louis-Edmond Hamelin, professor of geography at Laval University, described the concept of "northerness" as measured by such factors as physical geography, climate, vegetation, isolation, population density, and economic activity.[3] Hugh Brody, on the other hand, refers to the gradual expansion of the agricultural frontier, with the result that "north then, is the other side of the conveniently sliding divide. The 'real' north keeps moving north, but never ceases to exist."[4] A reverse description by the editors of *Nastawgan,* claims "the historic north moves southward as one moves back in time."[5] North can also be a state of mind, directly related to one's experience. From either perspective, the two words, north and wilderness, are often considered synonymous.

In recent decades, historians have attempted to explain the economic, physical and psychological impact of north on the nation's ethos. Initially, W.L. Morton described the Canadian Shield as an immense heartland affecting the character of the people, their mode of living and the economy upon which they depend. He later declared that "the comprehensive meaning of Canadian history is to be found where there has been no Canadian history, in the North."[6] Carl Berger argued that the belief that the North exerted a powerful influence on national character and identity originated from an Anglo-Saxon myth which promised future prosperity to a northern country, populated with people of northern races.[7] More recently, Robert Page wrote that southern attitudes towards the North were historically a combination of a romantic vision, "deeply implanted in the national consciousness," and one of "greed and economic exploitation," and that, even today, Canadians have retained "much of the traditional mythology, including its basic split between development goals and idealism."[8] Bruce W. Hodgins also described how conflicting images of north have persisted in Canadian historiography, causing confusion and debate as to the degree of influence and meaning.[9] Most scholars, however, agree that Canada's north has inspired national unity by creating a sense of unique identity in an American-dominated continent.

The role of the canoe in our northern heritage has also received increasing attention in the academic community as evidenced in the recently published *Nastawgan* and the illustrated history, *The Canoe,* by Roberts and Shackleton. In *The Canoe and White Water,* C.E.S. Franks claims that Canadians' "lack of appreciation of the arts of canoeing" stemmed from the fact that the fur trade had no substantial contact with the agricultural frontier. As a result, "white water canoeing was only a mythological, not a visible, fact in most of settled Canada."[10] The logic of this argument accepted, a further hypothesis to consider is one relating images of the canoe to the contradictions inherent in Canada's northern myths.

Every society has its own set of myths to explain its origins and character. While there may be personal connotations to perception and interpretation, it is the collectivity of similar attitudes that gives credence and strength to a myth. The same is true for symbols. The universality of acceptance may be measured by the degree to which these have been integrated into a nation's cultural framework, as reflected in folk songs and ballads, poetry and prose, art, theatre and dance. Despite the complexities of regionalism, there is a strong consensus that the various myths of the north have impacted on popular attitudes and perceptions to create a unique Canadian character and national identity.

Most northern myths were based on perceptions of land and climate, varying according to the cultural traditions of the observers. With qualification owing to overlap, several categories arise: the aesthetic and philosophical images; the frontier or nation-building myths, and "the north as homeland." All were rooted in first-hand experience, then molded by idealism, regionalism and the cultural baggage of new immigrants, and eventually transmitted to future generations through literature, music and art. The resulting "myth of the north," became an amorphous, obscure, yet constant theme in Canadian nationalism. When viewed as a whole, it is full of contradictions; when considered in its parts, it has been a source of celebration, pride and promise. The canoe plays a central role in several of these myths and thus shares some of the prestige and honour as a symbol of Canada's northern heritage.

The oldest perception of north is that of "homeland" belonging to the indigenous peoples. While there are many cultures and subcultures among the Indians and Inuit of northern Canada, they share similar attitudes towards the land as a result of their adaptation to what most southerners consider a hostile environment. To the Inuit, it is *Nunatsiaq*—the beautiful land. As described by Fred Bruemmer, who has lived and travelled extensively in the Arctic,

He (an Inuk) was part of it; it brought him sorrow and it brought him joy, and he lived in harmony with it and its demands, accepting fatalistically, its hardships, exulting in its bounty and beauty.[11]

The Dene of the Northwest Territories held similar beliefs. In the Athapaskan languages, there is no word for wilderness. Wherever they travelled, it was "home." In the words of one Dene, the land represented "the very spirit of the Dene way of life. From the land came our religion ... from the land came our life ... from the land came our powerful medicine ... from the land came our way of life."[12] The north as homeland was never "owned" in the sense of western man. The land belonged to the Creator and, in the Dene expression, was only borrowed for their children's children.

Quite naturally, canoes in their various forms were closely identified with the indigenous people who created them and who depended upon them for their existence. In the Arctic, the Inuit covered wooden or bone frames with sealskins to build their kayaks and umiaks. The woodland Indians utilized the bark of birch trees to fashion the sturdy craft required to traverse the lakes and rivers in search of game. Smaller trees naturally produced smaller canoes of different construction and with more seams, as in the case of the crooked canoe used by the Cree of northern Quebec. In the absence of birch bark, there were wooden dugouts, canoes fashioned from elm bark, or wooden frames covered by moose hide.

These vessels were objects of great pride and were often decorated with emblems to distinguish the owners. The art of canoe building was passed down through generations, with the design adapted to available materials and demands of the waterways. Quite apart from the primary utilitarian purpose, the canoe was also used in competitive sports and for ceremonial purposes. While it is true that, to the aborigines, the canoe and its various adaptations were considered "an extension of their home,"[13] their perception of being at one with the environment would include the canoe as an extension of oneself, a link to the natural world. As such, there was an attendant spiritual connotation. This was particularly highlighted among cultures which used the canoe to transfer their dead to the burial ground, or as a coffin on the premise that, in death, "a spirit canoe" would carry them into another life. Thus, to the many indigenous peoples of northern Canada, the canoe or kayak was identified more with individuals or families rather than with the physical environment.

Inevitably, it was the adoption of the birch bark canoe by European fur traders that inspired the more widely accepted association of canoe and north.   Although the beaver is undoubtedly the most popular symbol of Canada's fur trade, the voyageur canoe certainly ranks a close second. Just as the horse was considered as symbolic of the American western frontier, the canoe represented the north in Canadian history; both were means by which the Europeans initially penetrated the wilderness regions of the New World.   Subtle differences emerged later.

The canoe ultimately took on some of the legendary qualities of its masters. Just as one often refers to the image of "the solitary Indian and his canoe," the fur trade canoe became identified with the coureurs de bois who sought freedom and adventure in the wilderness. These recalcitrant entrepreneurs were considered of questionable character, despised by the missionaries and distrusted by officials, but they also represented adventure and challenge. Instead of conquering or attempting to civilize the wilderness, they sought to preserve it from encroachment by agricultural settlement. As a result, the colonists of New France acquired contradictory perceptions of the *pays d'en haut*: the image of a resource-rich but remote, hostile, and godless wilderness, yet at the same time symbolic of excitement and freedom, a place where one could escape the regulated society of the French regime and make a fortune in furs. The venerable birch bark canoe was the celebrated vehicle to freedom and adventure, and similarly the means of return to loved ones and family.

Following the Conquest, the voyageurs hired by the Nor'Westers gave further credence to established fur trade myths. These men toiled endlessly without complaint, proud of their strength and skill, joyous of their freedom and relative independence. After the amalgamation of the two major rivals, the North West Company and the Hudson's Bay Company, the term "voyageur" came to be commonly used to describe most participants in the fur trade, portraying a romantic image similar to that of the original coureurs de bois. As a result, the voyageur and his canoe became fully integrated into both English and French versions of our cultural heritage. According to the authors of *The Canoe*:

The voyageurs have left to history the image of a happy and carefree fraternity, always singing to the rhythm of their paddles, cock-proud of the finery they donned just before arriving at the trading fort, feasting like gluttons when there was food to spare, pushing on stoically when the pot was empty.[14]

The canoes themselves became virtual objects of art, crafted with care and decorated with the company crest and additional Indian or European motifs.

Much of our present knowledge of the fur trade canoes and their role in our heritage has come by way of the diaries of fur traders and missionaries. Their attention to detail, and desire to relate their impressions and emotional experiences have provided succeeding generations of writers and scholars with an authentic mirror on the past. An almost magical connotation was attributed to the voyageurs by a former Hudson's Bay employee, who described the thrill of hearing the "wild romantic song" and seeing a brigade of twenty or more canoes rounding a promontory, "half shrouded in the spray that flew from the bright vermilion paddles."[15] Less romantic accounts inform us that the canoes used by the voyageurs were not the 16- and 17-foot trippers of the 20th century but veritable giants such as the *canot du maître,* a 36-foot freighter weighing 600 pounds and carried by four men, or the *canot du nord,* which weighed only 300 pounds and was carried by two men. At the same time, visual images of these great canoes have been faithfully preserved in the paintings of John Halkett, Frances Hopkins and Arthur Heming, and others. If pictures are worth a thousand words, the legends of the fur trade canoes have been told and retold the world over, in galleries and private homes, and through countless reproductions appearing on posters, in books and magazines.

A number of French-Canadian folk tales focussed on the tragedies or heroic feats encountered in the fur trade. The characters and details of the plots were original, but adaptations of European fables were assimilated into some of the folktale "lessons." The tale of *La Chasse Galerie* is a classic example, and one which accentuates the imagery linking the canoe to the wilderness. Related to the stories of those condemned to eternal damnation for having sold their souls to the devil, one version describes the flying canoe as having transported lonely men from a remote northern lumber camp to their loved ones in Montreal. Alas, the canoe was sterned by none other than the devil himself, and its eager occupants paid dearly for their voyage.[16] Of significance here was the positive image of the canoe as a vehicle providing escape from a negative image: the fearful isolation of the north.

The folk songs of the fur trade are equally important in assessing the significance of symbols and myths. Singing and chanting in time to the dip of the paddles were means of keeping a steady pace and relieving the monotony of long stretches of lake travel, and the message varied to fit the mood or the occasion. Over time, folk songs go through many adaptations and revisions, both in words and tune. The origins of "The Masterless Men" are cited as a coureur de bois speech from *Welcome to New France*; translated, it reads:

We have slipped from the grip of the Church
We have travelled beyond the reach of the King
We are the children of the wind
We are the masterless men.

An English version written in the 1980s illustrates the enlargement of the imagery over a span of two centuries:

The paddles keep time as our voices ring out
And songs touch the furthermost shore
The rocks answer back with our laughing and singing
And we're off to the northwest once more.

We are the masterless men!
We harken to no one's command.
We roam where we please, cross the lakes through the trees,
We are the masterless men.[17]

Undeniably, the image of the voyageur canoe has evolved into a symbolic association with freedom, adventure, and the wilderness north.

While it is clearly evident that the canoe is central to our fur trade heritage, another link must be examined to explain its continued role in the enduring romantic myth of the north, one which reinforced the image of freedom, adventure, and escape into the wilderness, derived from the fur trade myths. By the early 19th century, the political and industrial revolutions in Europe gave birth to changes in social and intellectual perceptions. In Britain, the age of romanticism was accompanied by an increasing fascination with the relationship of man to his natural environment. It was the era of Wordsworth and Byron, of Turner and Constable—literary men and artists who began to express their perceptions in terms of either the "sublime," an accentuation of the mystery and grandeur of nature, or the "picturesque," denoting a harmonious relationship between mankind and nature. By the 1830s, American painters such as Thomas Cole adopted the "sublime" technique with emphasis on a hostile, forbidding environment; others such as Frederic Church, Albert Bierstadt, and Thomas Moran followed a few decades later, introducing a warmer, more inviting interpretation of the landscape. Canoes or boats, if appearing at all, were minuscule in relation to the surroundings.

Initially, the age of romance had little effect on Canadian authors. To Susanna Moodie, Catherine Parr Traill, Sir John Galt and other anglophone writers of the pioneer era, the frontier or "near north" inspired an image synonymous with hardship and challenge. With the exception of Anna Jamieson's description of her travels on Georgian Bay in the 1830s, rarely was there any mention of the fur trade. A more "picturesque" natural world was described with a focus on the foreground, on the flowers, trees and woodland paths, or in Gaile McGregor's words, a "Shaftesbury-Wordsworthian image."[18] In early French and English settler literature, the wilderness beyond was perceived as fearful and hostile, a perception that gave inspiration and substance to Northrop Frye's concept of Canadian's "garrison mentality." By contrast, a more aesthetic vision was ascribed to the Arctic by the raconteurs of the 19th century British admiralty explorations, especially those searching for the lost Franklin expedition. With the exception of the four overland attempts, the canoe is singularly absent from these narratives which clearly differentiate the Arctic from the more general term, north. Here, the kayak belonged to the Inuit; the sailing ships and their longboats to the Europeans.

Meanwhile, a quite different form of northern myth emerged in the years prior to and following Confederation, a national image which inspired Anglo-Canadians to new heights of self-confidence and expectation at a time when patriotic sentiments were at a feverish pitch. From the vision of a nation stretching from sea to sea grew the idea that "Canada's unique character derived from her northern location, severe winters and heritage of northern races," a notion that had its roots in a lecture entitled "We are the Northmen of the New World," given by R.G. Haliburton of the Canada First Movement.[19] For decades, this Darwinian concept became a recurrent theme in Canadian nationalist rhetoric with its attendant promise of future prosperity. Exploited to the fullest in the boosterism of the western expansionist movement, it appeared again as the main thesis in Vilhjalmur Stefansson's *The Northward Course of Empire* in 1922, re-emerged with new vigour in the mid-forties as part of the promotion of a "New North," and in Richard Rohmer's mid-Canada campaign. It was a popular myth, equally enduring as the aesthetic myth arising from the European age of romance, but its goal ultimately demanded destruction of the wilderness so revered by those who dreamed of freedom and adventure. Initially, the inherent contradiction was not readily apparent; to Canadians, the northern wilderness seemed limitless. More importantly, neither the pioneer nor later exploitation myths involved any direct relationship to the canoe.

The last half of the 19th century saw the emergence of new attitudes in the United States. The frontier myth which viewed land as an object to conquer was increasingly challenged in the published writings of an urban-based intellectual community. Just as Canadians had begun to look to their north as a source of future prosperity and identity, "wilderness" was declared a symbol of America's uniqueness in the western world. From this new perspective, unsettled lands were no longer considered fearful or alien, but rather places of beauty and a psychological counterbalance to the negative aspects of urban life. The works of American philosophers such as Henry David Thoreau, Ralph Waldo Emerson and Walt Whitman added to this interpretation by measuring the value of wilderness in terms of spiritualism and transcendentalism. It was definitely an urban-inspired idealism, arousing little sympathy among the residents of the frontier—a situation somewhat analogous to the resistance of white northerners to the present day environmental movement.

Once this new perception of wilderness gained general acceptance, it was only a matter of time until concern arose for its preservation. By now, the detrimental effects of clear cut lumbering were increasingly apparent in the eastern forests; thus, it was not surprising that American foresters, naturalists and the intellectual community subsequently joined forces in a campaign to stem the disappearance of natural wild lands. When the American western frontier closed rapidly toward the end of the century, the "conservation" movement gained momentum, as reflected in the founding of the Sierra Club in 1892, with transcendentalist John Muir as president. Efforts to preserve large wilderness areas as national parks were accorded the ultimate in political support when President Theodore Roosevelt adopted an active leadership role in the campaign. In his estimation, the preservation of wilderness was necessary to prevent loss of character and manliness through "overcivilization." City life, he claimed, would encourage laziness of body and mind.[20]

Of particular significance was the parallel rise of a wilderness appreciation cult in the United States and the growth of urban-centred canoe clubs in both countries. The Canadian tradition of canoe races began with Indians who were challenged first by the voyageurs, then by early settlers along the St. Lawrence and Ottawa Rivers, reportedly as early as the 1820s.[21] The canoe became increasingly identified with competition and regattas, first informally in the mid-19th century, then through various rowing clubs before the establishment of canoe clubs in the 1880s. Although American interest in paddling appears to have originated from the adventure concept of a wilderness experience involving camping, fishing, and hunting, by the time the American Canoe Association was founded in 1880, canoeing had become a highly competitive sport centred around urban boating clubs. The 1883 ACA regatta held on Stoney Lake in the Kawarthas intensified Canadian interest in international competition; it also introduced American canoeists to the lake country north of Toronto.[22]

Interest in competitive racing and canoe sailing would gradually diminish, but in the meantime American paddlers had discovered an ideal wilderness to rejuvenate the body and mind—the Canadian "north." The advantages of promoting tourism did not go unheeded in Ottawa or the provincial capitals. As a consequence, the Canadian conservation movement was more strongly influenced by the proponents of scientific forestry and tourism than by the wilderness appreciation and preservation aspects of its American counterpart. As such, it was not an intellectual or populist phenomenon, but one led by senior civil servants on behalf of lumber and recreation interests. Geographer J.G. Nelson argues that, not only did wilderness appreciation develop earlier in the United States, but in Canada "it seemingly appeared only rarely and then usually in the contained and conservative way typical of Canadian reaction to romantic or aesthetic ideas."[23] Nevertheless, the "back-to-nature" ideology slowly gained acceptance in Canada in the years prior to World War I, with the canoe heritage of the Canadian Indian forging the link and the impetus.

Meanwhile, in the United States, the wilderness cult had focussed on the far north much earlier than most imagined. By 1890, over 5000 American tourists had travelled by steamship to Glacier Bay in Alaska, to enjoy "a wilderness experience." A number of individuals also ventured into the Canadian far north, some seeking adventure and others hoping to gain scientific knowledge. Several went on personal expeditions, notably Frank Russell and Caspar Whitney, as did British adventure seekers Henry Toke Munn, Warburton Pike and David Hanbury. Following the tradition of the early explorers, these men travelled by canoe and dog sled; they also kept daily journals of their experiences, describing the hardships, the uncommon beauty, and the vastness of the landscape, with significantly more emphasis on wilderness appreciation than earlier accounts. In many instances, they were clearly following the "quest pattern" of the polar explorers which had its origins in the exploits of Prometheus and Jason in Greek mythology.[24] Few Canadians set forth, although countless numbers read the published narratives of the British and American adventurers. The canoe was central to these experiences and as such provided subconscious reinforcement of the philosophical rationale behind wilderness camping.

Any suggestion of Canadian apathy towards their north disappeared with the major discovery of gold in the Yukon in 1896. Roderick Nash argues that for the most part the

stampeders followed the same quest pattern of the northern
adventure-seekers in that most "sought the excitement of
wilderness rather than gold. They were not frontiersmen, so
much as city folks seeking a frontier experience."[25] In contrast
to the favoured American route by way of the Alaskan ports of
Skagway and Dyea, over the passes and down the Yukon River,
many Canadians attempted to follow the canoe routes of the fur
trade. Only a handful were successful in reaching their destination. Meanwhile, the armchair observers were caught up in
the magic of the gold quest, so vividly described in all manner
of fiction, guide books, autobiographies, poetry, art, and photog-
raphy. The image relayed was one of high adventure, intrigue
and mystery, challenge and hardship. It also gave substantive
evidence to the myth of northern resource wealth, but the role
of the canoe was only of secondary importance. Unlike the
prospectors in northern Ontario and Quebec, who depended almost entirely on the canoe for travel on the remote rivers and
lakes, the high mountain passes and fast flowing rivers of the
Yukon generally demanded alternative means to penetrate the
deep wilderness.

The resulting Klondike literature placed the Yukon on the
world map, notably through the immortal works of Jack London
and Robert Service. The latter, a young bank clerk from
Scotland, was particularly adept in describing the distinctive
lure and magic of the northern wilderness in his immortal "The
Spell of the Yukon."

There's gold and it's haunting and haunting;
    It's luring me on as of old;
Yet it isn't the gold that I'm wanting
    So much as just finding the gold.
It's the great, big broad land 'way up yonder,
    It's the forests where silence has lease;
It's the beauty that fills me with wonder,
    It's the stillness that fills me with peace.[26]

In these few lines, Service captured the magnetism, quest,
grandeur, isolation, and awesome spiritual quality of the northern wilderness. Rejecting the exploitation myth in favour of a
philosophical explanation, he claimed it was the image of
adventure and challenge in the land beyond, not the gold, that
lured the masses to the Klondike. Further clues to the origin of

his beliefs may be found in *The Ploughman of the Moon* which tells of his own canoe trip up the Rat River in the Northwest Territories, then down the Bell and Porcupine Rivers to the mighty Yukon.

After the gold rush subsided, only a few adventure-seekers continued to travel to the far north by canoe in search of excitement and fulfilment, but those who did still wrote and published narratives; many conducted lecture tours; a few admitted to being motivated by the arctic adventure stories read in their youth. Most experienced an emotional disorientation when re-entering the civilized world; as described by George Douglas after returning from two years in the Barrens, "the times had changed, the change in ourselves had no reference to them but made conformity to established usages more than ever, difficult."[27] Just as the escapades of the coureurs de bois represented a refuge from the regulated society of New France, a wilderness adventure was now clearly identified as an escape from urban society.

By the 1920s, American books and journals extolling the values of a wilderness experience had found their way into most Canadian homes. The "nature writers" had a definite purpose, described by one author as a means of encouraging discovery of "some beautiful and forgotten part of ... man's own soul."[28] For Americans, wilderness could be found in pockets throughout their land, in New Mexico, northern California, New England and the Everglades, but the canoe tradition figured most strongly in the northeastern states, as well as northern Michigan, Wisconsin, and Minnesota. In Canada, with the possible exception of the Maritimes, wilderness meant "north" of everywhere. In Gaile McGregor's view, "Canadians embraced enthusiastically a romantic cult of primitivistic wilderness worship" that, over time, created a deeply ingrained environmental perspective which "still exerts a disproportionate influence on Canadian thinking."[29]

Following in step with American trends, a number of Canadian authors adopted a similar emphasis on nature and wildlife. Adventures in wilderness settings quickly gained popularity: the works of P.G. Downes, Arthur Heming, and Grey Owl, as well as the unique wild animal stories of C.G.D. Roberts and Ernest Thompson Seton. Canadian magazines continued to carry articles describing various wilderness experiences, most accompanied by illustrations or photographs. Advertisements increasingly used pictures of wildlife, canoes, lakes, rocks and pine trees to promote various commercial products or services. Growing popularity of the wilderness ideal also provided the impetus for C.W. Jefferys, Tom Thompson, Emily Carr, and the Group of Seven artists to portray their images of mountains, trees, and water as symbols of Canadian nationalism: many set out by canoe to seek new sources of inspiration. The drowning of Thompson while paddling on Canoe Lake was tragic, yet ironically symbolic of the links between the artists, the canoe, and the north.

For many Canadians, the wilderness was more than a mental image, since with minimal effort, one could experience it first hand in the "near north." American money built 3-storey summer hotels, rustic lodges, fishing camps, and cottages in the Ontario and Quebec lake country. Canadians followed on their heels, to the Laurentians, the Muskokas, the Kawarthas, Temagami, along Georgian Bay, and on through the Lake of the Woods region to the Rockies. The ability to paddle a canoe was considered essential to enjoy a northern vacation, and wilderness canoe tripping inevitably became the ultimate experience in understanding the meaning of Canada. A 1915 article in *Rod and Gun* expressed the sentiment eloquently:

There is a secret influence at work in the wild places of the North that seems to cast a spell over the men who have once been in them. One can never forget the lakes of such wonderful beauty, the rivers, peaceful or turbulent, and the quiet portage paths, or the mighty forest of real trees. It is really getting to know Canada, to go where these things are. After having made camps along the water routes, one feels a proud sense of ownership of that part of the country, which must develop into a deeper feeling of patriotism in regard to the whole land.[30]

By this time the romantic image of "north" had spread into every aspect of the Canadian culture, in much the same way as the appreciation of wilderness was absorbed earlier into the American ethos. Youth camps for both the wealthy and less privileged sprang up in the lake country, providing an opportunity to learn the necessary prerequisites for a wilderness experience: swimming, canoeing, woodcraft, and survival techniques.[31] The campers also learned the ways of the Indian, his respect for nature, his legends and rites. New national and provincial parks were created while politicians began to talk more earnestly of the need to preserve wildlife. The message was carried throughout Canada and the United States, in school textbooks, by the Boy Scouts and the YMCA, in novels, sermons, hymns and art.

An example of the fervour and moral conviction behind the ideology is found in the 1918 edition of *The Tuxis Boys' Manual*. The purpose of the canoe trip was not simply to develop a strong physique and moral character but to see and understand the true meaning of Canada. A "camp log" written by John D. Spence outlined some of the potential benefits:

A brief return to the crudeness of nature; a brief renunciation of the artificiality of business and social life; a brief enjoyment of skies and lakes and rocks and pine trees at their freshest and best. Then, with firmer grip and steadier purpose, back to the work or the waiting, back to the rush and the bustle of the city, to brush shoulders with our fellows in whom we approve the good and censure the selfishness with greater charity because we have been ourselves brought nearer to the trust and truthfulness of our childhood.[32]

Significantly, the conscientious effort to educate the younger generation on the value of Canada's north was derived from convictions already held by an adult intellectual elite. To have experienced a wilderness canoe trip was the mark of an educated and enlightened gentleman.

Perhaps at no other time do we find the romantic image of the north so closely related to the canoe as in the popular literature, poems, and camping songs originating in those years, be it Pauline Johnson's "The Song My Paddle Sings," George Marsh's "The Old Canoe," or the venerable "Land of the Silver Birch." Perhaps maudlin by present-day standards, "To the North," appearing in *The University of Toronto Songbook,* seems to sum it all up:

Nor South, nor East, nor golden West,
Can match the Northland's rugged pride,
The North, the hardy North's the best!
To the North, to the North we go!
To the North, where the pine trees grow.

Then it's ho! for the gleaming paddle;

And it's ho! for the line and rod,
And the rushing fall, and the pine trees tall,
    And the waters bright and broad,
To the North, to the North we go!
To the North, where the pine trees grow.

During the interwar years, there was no question that the
northland and the canoe belonged together in the minds of many
Canadians. Still, although the canoe might conjure up images
of north, the reverse appeared to be less true.

The Great War appeared to have a sobering effect on
those dreams of untold wealth awaiting Canadians in their
northern wilderness. Although veteran prospectors still ventured forth, new mining technology and the use of the bush
plane gave an added advantage to company ventures backed by
greater financial resources. Even the discovery of gold on the
shores of Great Slave Lake in 1937 failed to rekindle the
enthusiasm of the Klondike years. In the cynical opinion of one
long-time resident of Yellowknife, "the Dawson rush was like the
careering gallop of a wild unbroken stallion, and the Yellowknife
rush, like the plodding of a cart horse."[33] Many still sought instant riches, but the stock market of the 1920s provided more
promising prospects with seemingly less risk and minimal physical effort. When it crashed in the fall of 1929, most Canadians
sought stability and security. Canoe trips offered a relatively
inexpensive vacation, but only a privileged few could afford
extensive time away from work if they were lucky enough to be
employed. By the nature of their professions, school teachers
and senior academics were among the more fortunate. Meanwhile, bush planes increased their penetration into the far north,
making access less of a challenge and the experience less unique.
The wilderness quality of the near north slowly diminished,
helped along by a growing American market for the Canadian
tourist industry.

Still, many Canadians continued to view the canoeing
experience as a link to their land and heritage. As Canadian
historian A.R.M. Lower observed after a canoe trip to James
Bay,

...only those who have had the experience can know what a sense of
physical and spiritual excitement comes to one who turns his face
away from men towards the unknown. In his small way he is doing

what the great explorers have done before him, and his elation re-
captures theirs.[34]

As such, the canoe trip was more than a holiday; it was a pur-
suit of one's heritage and so became a popular pastime among
the more intellectually oriented.

By the Second World War, the far north was still a subject
of curiosity, celebrated as an intangible influence on the nation's
character—"the true north, strong and free." The bombing of
Pearl Harbour, however, transformed the far off romantic image
into one of stark reality. Apart from new strategic significance,
the prolific wartime activities associated with the building of the
Alaska Highway, the Canol Pipeline, air fields and weather
stations aroused serious concerns about sovereignty and previous
government neglect. Pressures from influential civil servants
and private citizens for major changes in social and economic
policies verged on jingoism. The message was also contradictory
when repeated references to "a new north," the land of opportunity, or "opening of the northern frontier" were combined with
the suggestion that the lure of the north represented "something
inherent in the human heart and the human soul which re-
sponds to the appeal of wilderness."[35] One of the more stirring
speeches referred to "the frontier as a bastion of freedom, and
the North as a permanent frontier."[36] This image of north was
truly a nation-building myth based on advances in aviation
technology and potential resource development. Despite the
many references to wilderness, there was no place for the canoe
in this vision of the future.

Changes in perceptions of the north were inevitable.
Other interests such as tennis, water skiing, sailboarding and
computer science began to replace the traditional emphasis on
nature crafts and canoeing at summer youth camps. In the near
north, modern technology brought new roads, high speed motor
boats, hydro, television and the telephone. With increasing
urbanization, the natural world retreated further and further
north. The various myths of the north, and the canoe as an
instrument of its appreciation, appeared to have diminished
importance in the modern world of nuclear arms and satellite
communications, until the ecological and psychological value of
wilderness once again found a receptive audience during the
environmental movement of the 1970s, this time in direct conflict with the resource exploitation goals of the nation-building

ideology that threatened the destruction of the northern wilderness. As a consequence, the canoe, which still represents the wilderness ideal of north, might also be considered an "anti-symbol" of the progress-oriented myths. No longer essential to would-be exploiters, it is now the preferred vehicle of the preservationists who oppose major development in a manner ironically similar to that of the coureurs de bois centuries earlier.

In each myth, the north is measured in terms of value. Overriding all variants is the "core" myth, with an enduring quality that suggests the vast wilderness regions continue to impart a distinct character to the Canadian people and their institutions. The centrality of the canoe in the romantic image of a wilderness north is undeniable, yet perhaps less celebrated now than other symbols, owing to the contradictions in the myths. Still, for Canadians, the canoe stands today as a proud symbol of the freedom, adventure, exhilaration and tranquility to be found in the wilderness areas of northern Canada.

Notes

1 Walden, K. *Visions of Order: The Canadian Mounties in Symbol and Myth*. Toronto: Butterworths, 1982, pp 116 & 8-12. Walden has derived his premise from the works of Claude Levi-Strauss and other eminent scholars who have attempted to identify the role of myths in the modern world.

2 Roberts, K.G. and Shackleton, P. *The Canoe: A History of the Craft from Panama to the Arctic*. Toronto: Macmillan, 1983, pp 1-2.

3 Hamelin, L. *Canadian Nordicity: It's Your North, Too* (English edition). Montreal: Harvest House, 1978, pp 15-46.

4 Brody, H. *Maps and Dreams*. Markham: Pelican Books, 1983, p 57.

5 Hodgins, B. and Hobbs, M. (eds.) *Nastawgan: The Canadian North by Canoe and Snowshoe*. Toronto: Betelgeuse Books, 1985, p 1.

6 Morton, W.L. *The Canadian Identity*, (2nd edition). Toronto: University of Toronto Press, 1972, p 93; and "The North in Canadian Historiography," *Transactions of the Royal Society of Canada*, Series IV, Volume VIII (1970), p 40.

7 Berger, C. "The True North, Strong and Free..." in Peter Russell (ed.), *Nationalism in Canada*. Toronto: McGraw Hill Ryerson, 1966, p 5.

8 Page, R. *Northern Development: The Canadian Dilemma*. Toronto: McClelland and Stewart, 1986, pp 2 and 23.

9 Hodgins, B. "The Canadian North: Conflicting Images, Conflicting Historiography." Unpublished paper, 1980, Trent University, Peterborough, Ontario.

10 Franks, C.E.S. *The Canoe and White Water: From Essential to Leisure Sport.* Toronto: University of Toronto Press, 1977, pp 56-7.

11 Bruemmer, F. *The Arctic.* New York: Quadrangle, 1974, p 208.

12 The words of George Blondin, as quoted in *Denendeh: a Dene Celebration.* Yellowknife, NWT: The Dene Association, 1984, p 93.

13 Franks, p 8.

14 Roberts and Shackleton, p 201.

15 As quoted by R. M. Ballantyne, *Hudson Bay,* London, 1879, in Eric Morse, *Fur Trade Routes of Canada/Then and Now.* Toronto: University of Toronto Press, 2nd edition, reprint 1984, p 110.

16 Fowke, E. *Folk Tales of French Canada.* Toronto: NC Press, 1982, pp 77, 116-24.

17 Grant, J. in C. Grant (ed.), *Touch the Pioneers.* Waterloo: Waterloo Music Company, 1984, pp 28-9.

18 McGregor, G. *The Wacousta Syndrome: Explorations in the Canadian Langscape.* Toronto: University of Toronto Press, 1985, p 42.

19 Berger, C. "True North, Strong and Free..." p 5. Also see C. Berger, *The Sense of Power.* Toronto: University of Toronto Press, 1970.

20 Nash, R. *Wilderness and the American Mind,* (3rd edition). New Haven: Yale University Press, 1982, pp 65-117.

21 Cole, J. "Kawartha Lake Regattas" in Hodgins and Hobbs, pp 203-10.

22 For a more detailed account of the development of canoe sport see the essay by Fred Johnston in this volume.

23 Nelson, J.G. "Canada's National Parks: Past, Present and Future," pp 43-5; also K. Morrison, "The Evolution of the Ontario Provincial Park System," pp 102-7; both in Wall and Marsh (eds.), *Recreational Land Use: Perspectives on its Evolution in Canada.* Ottawa: Carleton University Press, 1982.

24 James, W.C. "The Quest Pattern and the Canoe Trip" in Hodgins and Hobbs, pp 9-10.

25 Nash, pp 284-5.

26 Service, R. *The Best of Robert Service.* Toronto: McGraw-Hill-Ryerson, 1963, pp 1-3.

27 Douglas, G.M. *Lands Forlorn.* New York: 1914, p 270.

28 Long, W.J. *Northern Trails.* Boston: Ginn, 1905, p 217.

29 McGregor, pp 51-52. The author also emphasizes that both British and American literature in Canadian homes far outweighed the presence of Canadian works, well into the mid-20th century. p 55.

30 Bocking, W.R. "A Canoe Trip," *Rod and Gun* 12(6), 1915, p 6. As quoted in J. Benidickson, "Paddling for Pleasure: Recreational Canoeing as a Canadian Way of Life" in Wall and Marsh (eds.), p 325.

31 Back, B. *The Keewaydin Way: A Portrait: 1893-1983*. Temagami, Ont.: Keewaydin Camp, 1983.

32 *Tuxis Boys' Manual for Older Boys*. Canada Young Men's Christian Association, 1918, pp 189-91.

33 Price, R. *Yellowknife*. Toronto: Peter Martin Associates, 1967, p 117.

34 Lower, A.R.M. *Unconventional Voyages*. Toronto: Ryerson, 1953, p 24.

35 Camsell, C. "Opening the Northwest," *The Beaver*, June, 1944, p 15.

36 Keenleyside, H. "Recent Developments in the Canadian North," speech delivered at McMaster Convocation, May 1949.

Canoeing and Gender Roles

William C. James

How easily we accept the myths of masculine prowess as applied to canoeing. I once took advantage of an offer in an Algonquin Park brochure and sought advice from a park employee on how to pack a pack. The young man gave some very useful general guidelines along the lines of not placing sharp articles so they would stick in your back. He also stressed how desirable it was to be able to get across a portage in a single carry. To accomplish this, the male should carry the canoe and one pack, while the female should carry a smaller pack. Because women are significantly weaker than men, he explained, they should not be expected to carry very much. I began to wish I had not asked for help.

I already knew of course that it is "easier" for one person to portage a canoe than two people (because, I guessed, the canoe somehow became lighter when carried by a single person). The person carrying the canoe should therefore make up for that relatively light assignment by carrying the heavier pack. Thus it came about that at the beginning of a mile-long portage on my first canoe trip in many years I found myself attempting to portage a canoe and a heavy pack. I believed that I had already compromised my masculinity by not carrying the heaviest available pack, the food pack (lots of canned goods in those days). But I did tie paddles and life preservers to thwarts and seats, all in the effort to complete the portage in a single carry.

In an earlier paper, "The Canoe Trip as Religious Quest,"[1] I began in this way, reflecting on my own experience and how the features of the classic paradigm of the heroic quest fit the testimony of various people about the canoe trip. One of the perplexing problems arose when canoe tripping was used as an initiatory rite, especially of the trial-by-ordeal variety, and especially in an all-boys school, to reinforce masculinity. I also developed a distinction between one kind of canoe trip that was indigenous, harmonious, adaptive—and female—and another kind that was immigrant, assaultive, intrusive,—and masculine.

This part of my earlier work demands more consideration. I am now inclined to think, for instance, that the model of the heroic quest derives basically and perhaps exclusively from male experience. The major question to tackle here is whether canoeing is an exception to the general picture of the relation between masculinity and sport as developed, for example, by Bruce Kidd.[2] He describes how the most popular sports in the nineteenth century were termed "the manly sports." Further, the qualities they developed—"courage and stamina, ingenuity, close friendships, and leadership"—were traditionally associated with the dominant norms of maleness.[3] Sports, he continues, have developed as male preserves, and thus, by "preventing girls and women from learning in the same context, sports confirm the prejudice that males are a breed apart."[4] But one must wonder whether canoeing should be seen within this context of the development of other modern sports as particularly masculine enterprises, or whether the development and history of canoeing is different or exempt from the general rule. Since we know that men and women canoe together, then canoeing is not—at least not always—an exclusively male or female preserve. What might that mean? For Kidd states: "The effect of sports is ... relational—they perpetuate patriarchy by powerfully reinforcing the sexual division of labour."[5] Considering this background, let us examine the evidence as well for a sexual division of labour among male and female canoeists.

In search of such evidence I checked several books on canoeing, in search of either women's contributions and understandings, or else portrayals of a masculine identification with the activity. Not very far into *The Canoe*, by Roberts and Shackleton, one reads the following account of the canoe's possibilities, seen in broadly historical terms, for enhancing its user's mobility:

(The canoe) put the fisherman out on the water and extended the hunter's range. It carried braves to war and was freight vessel for Indian traders. It was a vehicle for one person to cross a stream or for a migrant people to cross the continent.[5]

All of these appear to be basically male endeavours: fishing, hunting, making war, doing business, exploration, and migration. In the last chapter, entitled "The Modern Canoe," we learn how delayed, in both the United States and Canada, was the acceptance of women into canoeing organizations. Equally slow in coming was the participation of women in competitive canoeing events at regattas. The canoe has usually been associated with such male activities as hunting, and only occasionally with such female activities as food gathering, for instance the harvesting of wild rice, or with female competition in regattas (most often among native women), or in exploration in which women were at best passengers. Even the typical turn-of-the-century photograph of a woman in a canoe shows her seated amidships wearing her white dress, perhaps carrying a parasol.

Another set of possibilities may be represented by the discovery of what the "boat" in general symbolizes. It is, of course, in the first instance a vehicle, as the above range of activities suggests, that provides mobility. Another possibility finds expression in the boat as the "cradle rediscovered," and therefore the mother's womb. From Moses in the bullrushes to the pages of recent issues of *Wooden Boat* magazine, cradles have been made deliberately boat-like in form, or else boats are imaged as being like cradles.

"There is a connexion," states Cirlot in *A Dictionary of Symbols*, "between the boat and the human body."[7] This womb-like, cradling aspect of the canoe might be illustrated from Margaret Atwood's novel *Surfacing*, where one of the narrator's earliest memories is "lying in the bottom of the canoe" as her parents paddled. The canoe went backwards through rapids, but the narrator remembers, in spite of the danger, "the hush of moving water and the rocking motion, total safety."[8] Later, when she dives from the canoe in search of rock paintings, the narrator refers to the canoe as a "mediator and liferaft" as it hangs "split between water and air."[9]

One thinks, too, of the fact that people (men?) give boats and canoes women's names, or of the fact that in Maori mythology women are identified with canoes, in continuity with the womb aspect of the symbolism, because women ferry the precious cargo of new life from another world to this one. Here, the symbolism of the boat as cradle or womb and as vehicle come together.

Staying with *Surfacing* for a bit longer, the male-female distinctions inherent in the dualities of the symbolism of the canoe are perceptively and brilliantly contrasted in an essay by Rosemary Sullivan[10] in which she shows how the differences in the relationship to nature and to power in Canada and the United States are set forth in *Surfacing* and in James Dickey's 1970 novel, *Deliverance*. In *Deliverance* the white-water canoe trip taken by the four men who set out becomes an escape from the civilized and domestic world of women with its boredom and normality into the primitive and instinctive world of nature: "The flight into nature becomes a flight into a closed masculine world where a man can recover the heroic dimension normally lost to him."[11] By contrast, Atwood has the return to the natural world restore an individual not to the "god-like role of hunter" in which others are brought under the control of his will, but to a position in which the energy absorbed from nature restores one to the role of suppliant, bringing about a position not "of power, but of awe, the capacity to worship."[12]

Whereas Dickey has his characters discover no moral insight, but only an exhilarating freedom, a cult of sensation and the mythification of violence—a rape and three murders take place in the novel—Atwood's narrator undergoes self-scrutiny and reflection emerging finally in transformation of the self. As nearly as I can find, the canoes in Dickey's novel have few symbolic associations. They are seldom more than vehicles. The only possible exception occurs towards the end when Lewis Medlock, lying wounded and exhausted in the bottom of the beached aluminum canoe under the hot Georgia sun, tells Ed Gentry: "Go and get somebody. Anybody. I want to get out of this goddamned roasting oven. I want to get out of my own coffin, this fucking piece of tin junk."[13] That is as close as I can recall any character in the novel coming to an imaging of the canoes, and the imagery is negative at that. Otherwise they are as impersonal as the violence in the story.

As part of the attempt to define and examine gender issues in canoeing, and wanting to escape the limitations of my male perspective on the question, I enlisted the help of five female canoeists[14] by means of a questionnaire. I wanted to see if men and women described their experience of canoeing in different terms, if women felt that males' use of the canoe reflected a masculine code of sport, whether a traditional role division took place, for example, on canoe trips, whether the canoe was symbolized in male or female terms, and so on. My method of gathering data would be scorned by social scientists as unscientific, and the results dismissed as "merely anecdotal." So be it: I understand myself to be collecting and dealing with perceptions.

The women who responded to my questionnaire generally reported that they did not associate canoeing with the promotion of a masculine code of sport. The reasons varied: several pointed out that canoeing was exempt from the general connection between men and sport because it is an activity (unlike hockey, for instance) that is more inclusive of women. Someone indicated that canoes in racing competitions could promote that masculine code, or regarded fans of speedboats and water-skis as more likely to exhibit a macho mentality than male canoeists. Another associated not canoeing, but sailing, with men—chiefly on the basis of her personal experience, but perhaps also because of sailing being technical, expensive and intellectual. Women, especially single women, who generally have less financial resources than men, are likely to find canoeing the more accessible and practical way of getting on the water. One respondent said that she "fantasized that men who prefer canoeing would be the gentler, more nurturing, more sensitive, and responsive types."

Someone whose experience of canoeing was chiefly either solo, with children or with other women, reported that on several occasions a man who was an inexperienced canoeist came along as "the passive or subordinate partner," an experience she described as "neutral." On other occasions she had unhappy and "conflict-ridden" experiences when the man, though "less experienced and less skilled,... insisted on being 'skipper'." She writes: "Against my protests they led me into dangerous and uncomfortable situations. We argued constantly. The pleasures of canoeing were wiped out."

Another woman who paddled principally with her husband described canoeing as "an example of co-operation—complete partnership. At the best of times we were in tune with each other, the canoe, the elements—even the universe." In these two instances it would seem that the canoeing experience may reflect the already existing relationship between the particular couple, although perhaps intensifying it, for better or for worse. One person put it well: "An initial assumption of canoeing is, I think, that if people *want* to participate in this activity, they will do it in a way that invites mutuality."

It was observed by one woman that although it was not generally true in the groups she had canoed with, there were a few cases she could recall in which the men were "pushing harder to go further on a trip, or faster, as compared with the women." Male teenagers especially "have wanted to use the canoe to demonstrate their strength more than the girls would have." She went on to say that "the teen-aged boys also tended to assume that any male could paddle harder than females even though, in the specific situations they were in, the female 'counsellors' were actually paddling faster than they could."

Now of course one of the obvious points that emerges here is that all of my informants, who report that in their experience canoes have not been used to promote a code of masculinity, would know little of what goes on when canoeing takes place exclusively among males. That is, in the instances they are reflecting on perhaps canoeing has already been "feminized" by the presence of females. When a canoe trip is used as an initiation rite for adolescent boys, ostensibly to make men of them, the group leaders in their pre-trip pep talk made the "exclusion of females" a defining mark of the exercise. The boys were told that "mummy won't be along" to take care of them. Masculine self-reliance was being promoted: this was a trip not for girls, not for sissies, not for the weak, or faint-spirited.

As Walter Ong shows in *Fighting for Life*, men have always had to find ways of proving that they were not women. But it is a waste of time for women to prove that they are not men.[15] Since we all begin in the feminine world boys must differentiate themselves from the given backdrop of femininity through contest, challenge, and proving themselves to be men. Bruce Kidd writes: "Sometimes I teased my mother and sister to tears to confirm that I had succeeded in being different from them."[16] He goes on to say: "I would have been devastated if a girl had played on any of the teams I was so proud to belong to." The adolescent son of a friend of mine steadfastly refuses to go on a canoe trip if there are going to be girls or women along.

When Don Starkell headed off with his two sons on a canoe trip "that would take us further than anyone had ever gone by canoe,"[17] a 12,000-mile trip from Winnipeg to the mouth of the Amazon River, he worried that one of his sons, Jeff, had a less than total commitment to the trip. An aunt and uncle on his mother's side had told Jeff that if he wanted to leave the trip at any time he could stay with them. The elder Starkell writes:

I knew that if the trip was going to work we needed singleness of mind, not options. We'd even agreed to give up all but the most casual involvement with women for the duration of the venture. To do otherwise, I felt, would compromise our sense of purpose .... This trip was going to need total dedication if we were going to succeed.[18]

On the Starkells' trip the push is constantly on, the goal always before them, while major obstacles and discouraging setbacks threaten almost daily at times to end the expedition or kill them. Their trip stands, to paraphrase the book's subtitle, as a classic instance of the ultimate male canoe adventure. Their relationship to the environment is fundamentally adversarial; the relationship between Don and Dana Starkell, father and son, is also adversarial. Frequently a fight breaks out between them: Dana throws a tantrum, dumps food around or destroys equipment; Don wrestles with him, gives him "a sharp whack with the back of [his] hand." Then they apologize and continue. The elder Starkell finds all this "discouraging and wrenching": "Here we are, father and son, isolated in South America, 8,000 miles from home, and what are we doing?—fighting instead of supporting each other. I've reached a point at which anything that separates us is unbearable for me—far more draining than any of the other hazards on the trip."[19] But the goal—the successful completion of the trip—remains more important than the relationship between the Starkells, father and son.

As Carol Gilligan indicates, for males self-enhancement matters more than affiliation.[20] In one study she cites it was discovered that men, "like pious Aeneas on his way to found Rome, ... steady their lives by devotion to realizing their dream, measuring their progress in terms of their distance from the shores of its promised success."[21] The Starkells' journey to the mouth of the Amazon is measured in terms of miles achieved and miles left to achieve, with regular maps to gauge what has been accomplished and what is left to accomplish. Or, as Ong states: "In real life across the world, ceremonial physical contest between father and son—wrestling, boxing, dueling—helps to bring sons to normal maturity, establishing the friendly agonistic distancing the male psyche needs."[22] In the December 1987 issue of *Atlantic* novelist Philip Roth writes that it was imperative for him to leave home to go to college in order to avoid a fight with his father; he went, but they had the fight nonetheless.

Mothers and daughters do not do this. In fact, it would be difficult to imagine two women even wanting to attempt the kind of trip the Starkells made, given its length and duration, its goal orientation, and the continual measuring of distance travelled. The checking of the calendar, the emphasis on performance under stress, and the exclusive dedication and commitment to the task make this a male challenge of the adversarial kind. One of my female informants writes:

The reason it's been almost exclusively men who have opted to pit their wit and strength against the sea to cross it (or drown in it) and not women—is because women have the sense and the realization that it's a fight not worth fighting—that the sea has a strength neither mortal wit nor mortal strength can better; that one needs luck too. Furthermore, women don't feel a *need* to fight the sea. They can love it from the shore.

Or, as Walter Ong puts it, "There are no female Don Quixotes. A woman tilting with windmills or driven by impossible dreams is not a poignant figure. All real women have more sense. Not all real men do. Masculinity has something futile about it."[23] Ned Franks, in *The Canoe and White Water*, describes what he terms a "route march" kind of canoe trip in which the object is to travel over the distance between two points as quickly as possible, without time taken for the usual pleasures of canoe tripping—"for resting during the day, for looking at animals and scenery, fishing, or any of the other activities that should accompany wilderness leisure travel."[24] Franks judges that the "occasional route march" provides "a peculiar masochistic satisfaction," like that from being in 100-mile cross-country ski marathon or, one imagines, a triathalon.

One of my female informants whose experience of canoe tripping has been exclusively co-ed reports that she has been on trips "that had a real push-for-mileage ethic and those which did not." She contrasts two camps offering canoe trips, the one having a "more macho-, mileage-, and difficulty-conscious program and the (other) as being much more conscious of the social elements of a canoe trip—of its potential for developing positive relationships with others, teamwork, appreciating nature, etc." She observed that both sexes exhibited or participated in one ethic or the other, but that the first was designed and directed by a man, and the second by a woman. Further, she writes, "while I definitely prefer the less-mileage, more looking around kind of a trip—I have been caught up in the other approach when on such a trip. I think *everyone* feels a sense of satisfaction and pride upon finishing a long day with lots of mileage put on the water and portage—whether male or female—but there are some trips for which that seems to be the central theme and others for which it is not."

These words exemplify what Carol Gilligan calls "the different voice" with which women speak: nurturing, giving, caring, and generally expressing that relationships are more significant than individual achievement, self-enhancement, or the attainment of freedom and self-expression through separation.

In an effort to get at what could be termed the sociology of men and women and canoeing, I asked whether on canoe trips where men and women were both present there seemed to be a role division of labour: "Do men plan the trip, arrange the equipment, paddle and portage the canoe—chiefly—while women do the meals, look after the kids, are concerned about shelter needs, etc.?" Most of those who responded said that "the labour was quite evenly divided," that "there are overlapping roles," that "jobs of all kinds are shared," or that "canoeing was an example of cooperation and complete partnership." Beyond that it was commented that if one broke down who did what, "we'd find that some of the women did proportionately more cooking and some of the men did proportionately more portaging—but generally these jobs were shared and any unequal division of labour came out of individuals' preferences rather than an imposed division of labour." Another mentioned that the "lifting of very heavy

loads was usually done by, or at least, with assistance of men."
Another found that "men do tend to prepare certain kinds of
equipment at times, such as tents." And another, whose
canoeing in mixed company had been with her husband, stated
that he did the steering "but that seemed to work best—it
needed the strongest (physically) paddler." That last observation
was shared by another who had noticed that when she "paddled
with a couple, the man is often at the stern of the canoe." (It
might be worth pursuing further whether there is a kind of
hierarchy of seating in a canoe: assuming height and weight and
experience are roughly equal, do males readily share the stern
position with females?)

One person commented that her own needs for greater
security than many people meant that she was concerned for
"how the details of the trip will work *before* a trip." She tenta-
tively ventured the generalization that women might therefore
be more concerned with the food to be taken, knowing the route
ahead of time, and the assurance that "the trip is getting off in
an organized state." My own experience has been that I have
seen equal or even greater concern on the part of men, when
women and children were along on a trip, in regard to such details as route planning, the viability of the distance and diffi-
culties to be encountered, the safety and comfort of all. In fact,
I would think that one might see the same patterns if a family
were planning a regular vacation, by car, for example. The details and arrangements would fall to the one better adapted to
organization and arranging such things, regardless of gender.

Is there a kind of role reversal that takes place on canoe
trips, so that males take on tasks they might not normally do,
such as cooking, looking after children, setting up tents, preparing bedding, while women similarly take on jobs that would in
the ordinary world be left to men, such as lifting heavy loads,
engaging in strenuous physical activity over a long day? If so,
this would accord with my previous hypothesis about canoeing
providing access to another world set apart from the ordinary.
As the anthropologist Victor Turner states in *The Ritual
Process*, we live in fixed and in floating worlds. In the fixed
worlds we impose classifications to keep chaos at bay, but fail to
invent or discover. So we generate spaces and times, in rituals,
carnivals, and drama, for instance, to subvert the normative,
escape routine, and generate novelty. Such areas, writes

Turner, "are open to the play of thought, feeling, and will; in them are generated new models, often fantastic, some of which may have sufficient power and plausibility to replace eventually the force-backed political and jural models that control the centres of a society's ongoing life."[25] Seen in this way, then, canoeing can provide an "anti-structure" to challenge, correct, supplement, and perhaps overturn the structures of ordinary social life, including patriarchal structures.

A woman with experience as a counsellor with Camp Outlook, a program for city teenagers in difficult circumstances, or tending towards trouble with home, school, or the law, says that the program gives these boys a chance to see women—who on the canoes trips are active and sports oriented—in a different light from what they are used to. Such women may pose a threat to a value system in which women are seen as passive or as sex objects. Despite one's guess that many of these boys have been raised solely by working women, the canoe trip experience gives them an opportunity to see a blending of male and female roles "in cooking, planning, setting up camp, in sterning a canoe." She concludes: "This is therefore one way that canoeing *is* being used as an overall positive influence for incorporating masculine and feminine qualities."

Again, this topic invites commentary about the uses to which canoeing is put by males and females, or what it brings out in them that might be sex differentiated. Here I found a contrast in responses. One woman said she thought that in the exclusive company of females "there is more relaxation involved in canoeing, perhaps more observing of the environment and scenery." She continues: "This is therefore one way that canoeing *is* being used as an overall positive influence on incorporating masculine and feminine qualities." Someone else, however, saw the canoe more in instrumental terms, "as the necessary, important, and pleasurable means of getting where I wanted to go." But it seemed that for her, the destination (the wilderness) and not the vehicle, was thought of in mythological terms.

The third area investigated by means of the questionnaire is whether the canoe, considered as a symbol and given its shape and uses, had stronger associations with the male or female. I foolishly asked whether it was envisaged as phallus or womb, a question that provoked responses ranging from "both," to "I've never thought of the canoe as being one or the other," to "Oh really!" to "Good grief!! What kind of a mind do you have?" This last respondent went on to say that she too did not normally think of the canoe as either phallus or womb.

Now maybe I should leave bad enough alone, but my thought was to see what associations were there. I reasoned that canoes are long and narrow (typically 17 feet long and three feet wide!), that they are used in racing, hunting, and fishing, exploring territory, proving oneself, conquering rivers. Yet, they are also, like all boats, associated with the womb and cradle, as they ferry people from one place to another, surrounding, protecting, and enclosing. In fact, it might be wondered whether a division could be made of the uses of watercraft along male-female lines, as the Inuit do between the kayak (the man's craft for hunting) and the umiak (the boat for transportation of people and goods).

One person who said she saw the canoe as more womb-like said as well that "it could be seen as a phallus pushing into unknown—or known—territory. And it does sometimes produce moments of ecstasy—and sometimes terror—in both partners." For others, the canoe was identified, not with competition or conquering, but with "gracefulness, a moving ahead, but a calm quiet moving ahead," though not necessarily associated with a womb. Another woman commented that at times "my canoe was like an extension of my body—that if I handled my paddle properly and shifted my weight just so, canoe, paddle and I were all one unity, responding to the direction my brain wanted us to go. Is this a phallus-like perception? I wouldn't know."

Some of my own thinking has been that the canoe might have associations with the female because of its shape in profile. A colleague tells me that archaeologists have found crescent-shaped copper disks of native manufacture in northwestern Ontario. They cannot decide whether they are canoe symbols or lunar symbols. The ambiguity is challenging and fascinating. If lunar, then there may be a direct association with the moon as symbol of transformation (it dies and is reborn each month), and also as an ancient and universal female symbol because of the association of the moon with the menstrual cycle. Similarly, the canoe might be seen as a vehicle of transformation especially associated with the female.

I also paid attention to the practice of giving boats women's names, or of referring to them as "she" or "her." Is this so, as one woman suggested, men can love them without guilt? And, if canoes are seen as female, is this a male propensity? Charles W. Gordon, who under the pen name of Ralph Connor was undoubtedly Canada's best-known novelist around the turn of the century, describes in his autobiography how he once expressed hope of learning about the canoe in a few days. His experienced partner retorted: "If you live a hundred years you'll never learn everything about a canoe. She's as full of whims and quirks as any other female thing."[26] Gordon declares that the "mysteries" of the canoe are "one of the tricks she has for making you love her,"[27] and a little later says that the canoe added to his "psychological education" by teaching him that canoes, like other "things of the female gender," will "not stand bullying."[28] The patronizing tone is typical of the era as males discuss management techniques for handling the mysterious, quirky, unpredictable, and capricious world of female things.

One woman expressed her strong objections this way:

... when a boat is talked about as feminine, generally the speaker indicates how he *controls* the boat. The boat is subject to his commands, it's performing for his purposes, he's using it to further his ends, etc., etc. When boat, feminine, is associated with being one's possession, one's servant, one's useful instrument, etc., I don't like that. ...

But, she says,

I don't mind a boat's being conceptualized as feminine when the sailor in question refers to his boat as a companion, or help-mate, as something he works *with* (not simply uses), as something he appreciates because it protects and holds him and isn't just a thing he bends to his superior will. It's okay if his boat is something that enhances his life, is an active partner in fulfilling him, brings him joy and is appreciated for this.

It is intriguing to notice how Cree canoe builders at Great Whale River imaged the canoe in the songs they sang while building. Typical might be a song that reiterates, "The female loon is guiding me safely on the water," or "the baby duck is taking me along." Over half the songs collected "refer to creatures which display proficiency in the water, whether birds, fish, or animals."[29] Some songs may be based on the myth of a magic canoe, while in another the canoe is a "man" of whom the builder is proud, or else the canoe is like a woman who dances before him on the waves, or once again, in a positive image of paternity, the builder's pride in his craft is likened to that of a father towards his growing child.

As a final question I asked my female informants how the feminine values and characteristics of canoeing could be incorporated alongside the masculine ones, actually a paraphrase of a question I found in a recent issue of the Canadian Outward Bound Wilderness School *Journal of Education*.[30] Outward Bound schools all over North America are currently reconsidering their motto and philosophy, perceived by many within the organization as promoting a macho image to the neglect of "receptive, yielding, cooperative side of the Self."[31] I was asking on the assumption that women's experience of canoeing has not been articulated as often or as fully as men's, and that we all could be enriched and our experience deepened if those perceptions were articulated. Several women did not like the question because of its (to me unconscious) assumption that canoeing was a male sport. One person responded that she saw canoeing as a "couple-oriented thing," a "romantic symbol as well as an adventure symbol." She spoke of the romance of "peaceful companionship alone in the vastness—just the two of you midst the glories of the great outdoors."

One woman suggested simply that the female contribution to the understanding of canoeing would be to "substitute cooperation for competition." Another urged that "the mentality of 'conquering' lakes and rivers must be defeated and canoeing enjoyed by both sexes as a sport and for pleasure." Still another objected to "chopping up the experience of canoeing into male and female components. That diminishes it." She wrote: "Canoeing is wonderful—joyful, self-affirming, expansive—and one very good reason why this is so is because it allows people to be *whole*—not divided into gendered categories, as most of society's institutions and activities require." Though this woman said that "generally I'm interested in analyzing anything in terms of gender categories, and trying to relate what may be wrong about something to its masculine characteristics," she declared that she "won't be part" of gendering canoeing. This response may amount to another way of saying that canoeing is to stand outside the normal patterns of everyday social life—as anti-structure to structure.

I will give the final word to one eloquent response to the question of how feminine values could be incorporated alongside masculine ones:

Slow it down. Don't have the distance covered and the number and length of portages be the only measure of success. There should be time and energy at the end of each canoe day for other things besides a quick meal and crashing out. Chances for quiet, private time; close-up looking time; hiking time; swimming time; water fights and digressions; star gazing; let's-stay-here-another-day-time; canoe sailing; good meals; floating lunches and basking in the sun. There should be a focus on the social aspects of a canoe trip—on the times shared together, as a group or in one-to-one situations. In the canoe, on the portage, at the fire. Having a bit more time at the end of a day (and/or in the middle of it) allows for private time to be alone, to find a quietness for whatever your soul is needing then: to walk feeling the moss under your feet; to crouch watching the waves lap the evening shore or an ant carrying a wasp wing over the uneven ground; to write; to think or *not* think; to wonder. I think it is these moments of wonder and awe and joy during those quiet times alone on a canoe trip that I value most. Just you in a secluded spot and the sky, and the greens and blues of the setting sun and the knowledge that you are a part of it, but such a small part of it, overwhelmed in the joy of the enormity and power and beauty of it. It makes me cry just to sit here in my living room and think about it. It's time for a canoe trip...!

These comments encompass both the social and individual features of canoeing, though even the solitary aspects of canoeing are social to the extent that they incorporate a relationship to the natural world. Like the narrator of Atwood's *Surfacing*, here is a person who finally comes to nature as pilgrim and suppliant, not as hunter or conqueror, and whose words are an example of how the female experience of canoeing may enrich and correct, challenge and complement, deepen and transform the male experience.

Notes

1 James, W.C. "The Canoe Trip as a Religious Quest," *Studies in Religion* 10(2) Spring, 1981, pp 151-66. And also "The Quest Pattern and the Canoe Trip" in Hodgins, B. and Hobbs, M. (eds.) *Nastawgan: The Canadian North by Canoe and Snowshoe.* Toronto: Betelgeuse Books, 1985, pp. 9-23.

2 Kidd, B. "Sports and Masculinity." *Queen's Quarterly.* 94(1) Spring, 1987, pp 116-31.

3 Kidd, p 119.

4 Kidd, p 121.

5 Kidd, p 120.

6 Roberts, K. and Shackleton, P. *The Canoe: A History of the Craft from Panama to the Arctic.* Toronto, Macmillan, 1983, p 2.

7 Cirlot, J. *A Dictionary of Symbols.* Second Edition. London: Routledge & Kegan Paul, 1971, p 30.

8 Atwood, M. *Surfacing.* Don Mills, Ontario: General Publishing, Paperjacks, 1973, pp 17-8.

9 Atwood, p 141.

10 Sullivan, R. "*Surfacing* and *Deliverance*," *Canadian Literature*, 67, Winter 1976, pp 6-20.

11 Dickey, J. *Deliverance.* London: Pan Books, 1971, p 9.

12 Atwood, p 13.

13 Dickey, p 199.

14 My thanks go to Sarah Morgan Balint, Helen Mathers, Danielle Michel, Ruth Studd, and Eleanor Zegers for their generous participation.

15 Ong, W. *Fighting for Life: Contest, Sexuality, and Consciousness.* Ithaca: Cornell University Press, 1981, pp 63-4.

16 Kidd, p 258.

17 Starkell, D. *Paddle to the Amazon: The Ultimate 12,000-Mile Canoe Adventure.* Toronto: McClelland & Stewart, 1987, p 16.

18 Starkell, p 210.

19 Starkell, p 207.

20 Gilligan, C. *In a Different Voice: Psychological Theory and Women's Development.* Cambridge: Harvard University Press, 1982, p 169.

21 Gilligan, p 152-3.

22 Ong, p 85.

23 Ong, p xx.

24 Franks, C.E.S. *The Canoe and White Water: From Essential to Leisure Sport.* Toronto: University of Toronto Press, 1977, p 139.

25 Turner, V. *The Ritual Process: Structure and Anti-Structure.* Ithaca: Cornell University Press, 1977, p vii.

26 Gordon, C. *Postscript to Adventure: The Autobiography of Ralph Connor.* New York: Farrar and Rinehart, 1938, p 49.

27 Gordon, p 50.

28 Gordon, p 66.

29 Taylor, J. G. *Canoe Construction in a Cree Cultural Tradition.* Ottawa: National Museums of Canada, 1980, p 32.

30 Suchman, N. "A Letter to COBWS," *Journal of Canadian Outward Bound Wilderness School Education* 3(1), June 1987, pp 6-7.

31 Wilson, T. *Outward Bound.* Script for CBC Sunday Morning, 13 September 1987, p 4.

Canoe Irony:
Symbol of Wilderness,
Harbinger of Destruction

Bruce Hodgins

We enlightened few clamour in fossil-fueled airplanes and petrochemical canoes, eating plastic-bagged food from aluminum dishes, to be the last to see the wilderness as it is. Perhaps what frightens us most about losing wildness, what drives us to become keepers of the garden, is that we recognize the irony in ourselves.[1]

For many, the canoe is the most appropriate symbol of the Canadian heritage. And the canoe involves canoeists. Pierre Berton claims that, symbolically, making love in a canoe is the most Canadian act that two people can do.[2] But the Canadian mythology or belief system about the canoe is nearly always linked to wilderness. "The canoe, the snowshoe, the wilderness and the North are inextricably entwined with each other and with our Canadian heritage."[3] Yet, if the canoe was deeply significant in creating the transcontinental Canadian nation bordering three oceans, the canoe simultaneously played a major role in destroying and reducing wilderness. Today, the canoe both helps to sustain and to threaten the wilderness and semi-wilderness which survives.

Most of us use bush planes in connection with our deep wilderness canoeing expeditions. Of course we do. It could hardly be otherwise, but listen to this announcement in a current issue of *Explore*: "Flying can enhance your recreational fun. It increases the time you spend in an area, saves tedious two-way trips, and opens up remote back country."[4] That made me blush! Nevertheless, despite an eloquent admonition from William James[5] concerning linear rather than circular trips, I still intend to organize and take such one-way canoe trips. But now I will do so with a little more humility.

Today, most Canadian canoeing is recreational. Many of us would assert that it is usually meaningful, aesthetically fulfilling and ecologically sensitive recreational canoeing. Admittedly, these modifiers are not necessarily present in the highly competitive, highly structured and technically oriented canoe racing sports which tend not to take place in a wilderness environment. But with these large exceptions, canoeing, certainly canoe tripping and lake water canoe cruising, tends to involve in varying degrees a quest for wilderness or at least semi-wilderness. It also involves a search for high adventure or natural tranquility or both. These activities are an integral part of Canadian culture. Bill Mason asserts that the canoe is "the most beautiful work of human beings, the most functional yet aesthetically pleasing object ever created," and that paddling a canoe is "an art" not a technical achievement.[6] That certainly means culture.

The early recreational canoeists, those around the turn of the century, sought out wilderness or what they then called the unspoiled bush. There was more of it then than now and much more close at hand or near to the rail lines. The relatively unsung trippers of that time experienced this aspect of the central Canadian heritage in accessible bush throughout the districts of Haliburton, Muskoka, Algonquin and even Temagami and Kipawa. They also read about the high canoeing adventures in the far north of men such as Warburton, Pike, the Tyrrell brothers, Ernest Thompson Seton, David Hanbury, George Douglas, and of women such as Mina Hubbard and Lady Clara Vyvyan. They vicariously shared the experiences of these great wilderness travellers. They lamented the shrinking wilderness. Furthermore, Tom Thomson and the Group of Seven were canoeists as well as artists when they painted their way into the centre of our heritage. The same goes for poets like Archibald Lampman, on the Lievre or in Temagami. Nearly always, the act of canoe tripping had something to do with wilderness, the beaver, the haunting call of the loon, and northness. For many Canadians, the canoe was the vital link between wilderness and culture.[7]

To a considerable degree, much of this country was put together, in the early years, by the canoe and by people who canoed. The canoe was the principal mode of travel, and the main inland commercial activity of the time involved a critical role for the canoe and the complex transportation network built around it. The fur trade empires were canoe-based ones. The continual interaction of people affects and modifies culture. People also interact with their environment and modify it. We now know that even aboriginal people modified their environment, altering it substantially by their use of fire, by new hunting techniques or, in southern Ontario, by agriculture. And the Indians used the canoe for warfare as well as for making love. Nevertheless it can still be asserted that the ecosystem, in the aboriginal eras of our past, remained more or less intact; the land remained what we now choose to call wilderness. Wilderness is thus a relative not an absolute term. Wilderness survived the presence of human culture, including the use of aboriginal canoes.

Though threatened, wilderness also survived the commercially-oriented fur trade canoes. The Indian-based, French diplomatic and fur empire of the interior was not a settlement empire. The French did not concentrate, as did the Anglo-American and the Spanish-American empires to the south, on rolling back the frontier. Instead, they concentrated on preserving a modified Indian way of life and a natural habitat for beaver, otter and mink. But the French often referred to the land above Lachine as *la ferme*, so there was some ambivalence. Were the French involved then in acts of preservation or of conservation? Certainly their aims were decidedly anthropocentric and far from altruistic. Their aims were imperial and exploitive of the natural environment and its aboriginal peoples. But they wanted wilderness and beaver to survive.

It has been said that, if the economy and culture of the American South was made on the backs of black slaves in the cotton fields, then Canada as a nation was first made on the skins of beaver transported by canoes. As they died prematurely, so we became a nation.

Champlain, our first governor and one of the first Europeans to be transported through the classic canoe country of Southern Ontario, did not much like what he saw. He detested the blue lakes and rocky shores of the Thirty Thousand Islands and the rest of the shield country. He much preferred the rolling landscape of what became the bucolic fields of the lowlands. But he came to see the importance of the shield-based fur trade. Then those semi-outlaws, the coureurs de bois, who lived and traded with the Indians, became the great canoeists of the day. But the French-organized, canoe-based fur trade was still dependent upon rapacity and cupidity. We now know that by 1700 the French fur business was operating collectively at a loss. It was an instrument of skillful royal diplomacy with Indian nations. The French Crown had decided that, for geopolitical reasons, the agrarian-based Anglo-American empire could not be allowed to take over the continent north of the Spanish interests. Hence the English would have to be hemmed into the seaboard by a network of alliances with inland Indian nations. These nations wanted European goods. So the fur trade had to continue. It could only continue with the use of the canoe.

The fur trade, like contemporary Canadian softwood lumbering, was subsidized for reasons of state. The canoe would remain almost the sole means of travel through this huge un-official, unowned empire, and the French crown would do all this with only a couple of hundred roaming French subjects actually involved with the Indian nations. Feeble forts were established. From these small outposts, linked to one another by the canoe, European culture spread out, shrinking and modifying the wilderness.

Meanwhile, to the north, the Hudson's Bay Company was establishing a much weaker mercantile empire, one which for a time would seem to triumph but which in the end did not survive. Modern European-Canada emanates out from the St. Lawrence, not from Hudson Bay, not from York or Moose Factory or Fort Albany. Until challenged after the conquest, Hudson's Bay Company traders tried to stay near the Bay and persuade the Indians to come downstream annually to trade. For several generations, the system worked. But the effect on the culture of various Indian nations was phenomenal. Various groups, even nations, that had been prairie-based became professional canoeists transporting goods back and forth for what amounted to a commercial fee. For both fur trader and Indian paddler, it was a job alternately full of adventure and boredom. Then, when challenged in the late 18th century, the employees of the Bay, men like Samuel Hearne and others, themselves moved inland—by canoe and snowshoe.

That challenge came from Scottish and American traders who had set themselves up in Montreal in the 1760s, men who ultimately formed the Northwest Company. They employed a French Canadian and a Métis labour force of expert but over-worked canoeing voyageurs. The exploits of the voyageurs be-came, in myth and saga, those of the heroic age of romantic but commercial canoeing. The age itself lasted only two generations, from the 1770s to 1821. But what an impact it had on our later culture. This was the era of the great canoe brigades, the 35-foot *canots du maître* and the 26-foot *canots du nord*, the *chansons* and the costumes. It was also the age of portage-induced hernias and canoeing-related drownings. This huge fur empire encompassing much of the central North and Northwest of modern Canada, left out Toronto and parts of Southern Ontario that were not contiguous to the Ottawa Valley.[8] It also left out the Maritimes. This would have great significance for the future because the imperial centre of Canada is now Toronto, and Torontonians can only vicariously link their past to a canoeing heritage.

Within a few decades the competition between the two "British" fur empires became intense and destructive. The struggle was fought out in the centre of today's more remote recreational canoe country, south of James Bay and on the Churchill, Clearwater and Athabasca watersheds. Blood flowed. Bodies dropped over gunwales. Competitive fur prices rose, but so did the quantity of the furs trapped. The environment came under strain. Canoe routes became overcrowded. Vast areas were trapped out. The trees and the waterways remained, but not many animals. In the heroic age of the canoe brigades, the wilderness and its wildlife were on the verge of severe shrinkage.

Then came that momentous year, 1821. To canoeists, that year and 1870 should be more important than 1867, the year of Confederation. In 1821 the weaker concern, the Hudson's Bay Company, bought out the stronger concern, the Northwest Company. No longer did the great canoe brigades continue to paddle up the Ottawa River. The wide portage trails began to grow over. Canoe travel out of Montreal did continue. It served the upper Ottawa Valley including Temiscaming, the French and the Sturgeon river valleys and, at times, the La Cloche area of northern Georgian Bay. The Ottawa-Huron route was also the route for the fast express canoes from civilization to the Northwest, carrying communications and important personages like the Hudson's Bay Company Governor Sir George

Simpson and his secretary, Hopkins.   More importantly, for symbol and myth, an express canoe carried his wife, Frances Hopkins, the magnificent artist of the great canoes.   But for the Northwest over the next sixty years, the trade centred again on Hudson Bay, controlled by a declining monopoly threatened not from "Canada" (that is, Montreal) but from the northern United States.   The agents of the Bay, wherever possible, converted canoe travel into York boat and barge travel.[9] The Hudson's Bay Company was not strong on sentimentality or concern for heritage.   The Bay servants did, however, expand the canoe routes far into the Yukon and the Oregon country and to the lands in between.   The Red River valley and the buffalo herds became respectively a farm and a source of livestock for the burgeoning work force of the fur trade.   By 1863, in its southern territories (but not in its northern ones), the Hudson's Bay Company had become more interested in real estate than in its traditional trade.   Often, when it saw the advances of settlement it urged its agents to trap the animals into extinction.   In 1870, for a price paid by Canada, the Bay surrendered its imperial claims which were then transferred by the Crown to the young Dominion.   In a sense, 1821 had been reversed.   The posts and canoe routes focussed on Hudson Bay declined.   In the European settlement of the West that was to follow, the canoe played only a subordinate, transitory role.

Nation building involved the subduing, or destruction, of the wilderness.   In this process, within what became Canada, the canoe was a major active agent.   A symbiotic relationship had developed between the canoe and wilderness.   In a sense, one fed on the other.   When the wilderness declined or shrunk, the canoe lost its commercial significance and went into decline.

Farther north, in the east and west, the canoe had continued to be important.   It was used for the most significant exploration of the interior.   Indeed, great fur traders had themselves been major canoeing explorers; Sir Alexander Mackenzie, Simon Fraser and David Thompson are perhaps the most famous.   But coterminously came other kinds of canoeing explorers, especially men such as Sir John Franklin on the Coppermine and the Mackenzie watersheds in the 1820s, and Sir George Back, with Franklin on his early trips and in the 1830s, on the greatest of the barrens rivers, that remote one which still bears his name.[10] Many of these expeditions were financed, for a variety of reasons, by the British Navy. Both Franklin and Back were great wilderness travellers, the latter much better than the former, and they tried to take civilization with them. They had very different views but both were negative about aboriginal culture and neither saw any future for wilderness—unless the land was otherwise useless to humankind.

In 1837, the Upper Canadian government financed three great canoeing expeditions between Georgian Bay and the Ottawa valley. They were intended to determine a potential route for a commercial transportation corridor from the upper Great Lakes to the Ottawa. An aging David Thompson led the southern trip on the Muskoka-Ox Tongue-Madawaska route.[11] The northern one was led by David Fraser via the Sturgeon-Temagami-Matabitchuan route.[12] The middle one on the Magnetawan-Petawawa route remains unheralded. Certainly, the northern and southern parties grumbled and deprecated wilderness and rapids. Thompson said of the Muskoka that "all is desolation and very little frequented by the Indians" while the Madawaska was full of terrible rapids, a river "impracticable to improvements." Fraser was appalled by the obstacles on the Temagami River, with its granite shores, "all craggy and broken," although he liked Lake Temagami's fishing and its "deep and beautifully clear" water. He commented that the land to the northwest, not yet seen by a European, and now called the Lady Evelyn Wilderness, was even "worse." If their missions had been fruitful, large accessible wilderness areas important to paddlers today would probably have been destroyed. Ultimately the route chosen was even farther south, the more bucolic Trent-Severn Waterway. But even today, some in North Bay and Premier Robert Bourassa in Quebec still dream of "improving" the French-Mattawa road by creating a canal linked to damming James Bay and reversing the flow of the Harricanaw River.

Immediately before, but especially in the decades following Confederation, the canoe was the principal means of travel for the great exploration and charting work of the Geological Survey of Canada. While excellent histories of that organization exist, the role of the canoe at its centre remains episodic rather than systematically described.[13] The purpose of these voyages of discovery which were paid for by the taxpayer was to inventory mineral and other natural resources of the remote, unsettled areas of the new nation, with a view to the imminent development of the more valuable ones.   Under the Geological Survey's direction, the rivers and lakes of Northern Ontario and Quebec were canoed and described in published detailed trip reports.   So were several rivers of the Northwest Territories.   The most famous expeditions were those led by the Tyrrell brothers, by William Ogilvy and, farther east and earlier, those led by Robert Bell and A.P. Low.

The ultimate purpose was development; this meant the destruction of wilderness, and often its wildlife habitat.   The agent of that destruction was the canoe, paddled by excellent and dedicated wilderness travellers.   What did these men (no women were hired) think they were doing?   Most, like the Tyrrells, clearly loved the solitude and awesome space of the northern wilderness.   That was why they came back year after year.   For a few, it was only a job leading to an administrative post in Ottawa.   Regardless, their lives were in conflict.   They were vital agents of urban development, agents of the southeast penetrating the remote reaches of the north for imperial rather than local or aboriginal purposes.   They were harbingers of change.   They were not agents of the conservation movement, to say nothing of later environmental movements.   Nevertheless, they often sounded like what Bill Mason calls the dangerously but happily addicted recreational canoeist of recent decades. Rarely did they talk about this dichotomy.   J.B. Tyrrell, himself, was ambivalent about wilderness.   He loved it in one sense, yet was committed to subduing and reducing it.   At times he longed for "a quiet home in the country, within easy reach of the city, from which one would not be obliged to wander off into the wilderness every year."   He later became a mining executive in Northern Ontario.   In his old age he was incredulous that anyone might want to repeat his canoeing adventures on the remote Dubawnt.   "Why on earth would you want to do that?   You can go there by plane, you know."[14]

When the Mounted Police abandoned horses for canoes and snowshoes, the story was similar.   They canoed through the far Northwest, bringing the rules of southern Canada to remote Indian and Inuit communities, and showing what passed for the Canadian flag in order to enhance our national sovereignty over remote landscape and alien cultures.[15]

The role of the canoe in the Northern Ontario mineral boom and, to a degree, the forestry boom at the beginning of this century, also fits the pattern. In 1900, the government of Ontario financed ten exploratory canoe trips which traversed much of what was then Northern Ontario, repeating and expanding the work of the federal Geological Survey and Ontario's tripping stipendiary Magistrate Edward Borron.[16] The reports make fascinating reading from a canoeist's point of view.[17] They foretold in general terms much of the development which was immediately to follow in Northeastern Ontario. When the prospectors came, they too arrived first by canoe and snowshoes. They had little concern for the environment; they wanted development and the fast buck. Often, these canoeists burned, rather than harvested, the pine forests.[18]

The early unsung recreational canoe trippers certainly were searching for wilderness.[19] They also wanted wilderness conserved or preserved in accessible areas. Usually, they were allied to the forest interests. Both groups—and some were the same people—wanted to keep out agriculture and urban development and wanted to conserve headwaters. They even shared the same journal—*Rod and Gun in Canada*. They helped to lobby for Algonquin Park, for the Temagami Forest Reserve and for what became Quetico. By the late 1920s many were connected with or had been connected with youth camps that had specialized in canoeing and canoe trips. They wished to preserve their beloved waterways.

Yet these largely unsung recreational canoeists played a major role in opening up the Old and Near Norths of Ontario and Quebec. Many camp counsellors graduated into cottage owners. Together they pushed for more roads to recreational lakes, more cottage properties, the wider expansion of hydro into the bush, and for better highways to cut the time from the southern cities to the shrinking and more accessible semi-wilderness. In some of the youth camps, sectarians used the wilderness, but not to teach about wildlands or the environment. Instead, they used the bush to isolate the children briefly from urban life so as to shape them in ways totally unrelated to an environmental ethic, more in line with their special way of dealing with that expanding urban life. Other camping leaders used wilderness to teach the male leaders of tomorrow macho roles which involved taming, subduing or destroying the wilderness.

Even into the late 1950s, one shudders at the environmental damage from camping practices which we as canoeists condoned, tolerated and practised. Indeed, the early recreational canoeists who loved and sought the wilderness were agents of its destruction.

Some will argue that the role of these recreational canoeists in a diminishing wilderness could not have been otherwise. John Livingston half seriously argued in the early 1970s that, if you wanted to destroy an area, you should make it into a park; that everyman's wilderness was a contradiction in terms. He also emphasized the crucial distinction between business-oriented resource conservation, on the one hand, which he deprecated, and wilderness preservation on the other, which he championed.[20] The canoeing recreationist was confused about where he or she stood in that issue.

But by the 1970s, leading recreational canoeists themselves were more introspective and clearer about their responsibilities. The "woodsman's code" and "no trace camping" were promoted—though the latter clearly was difficult to achieve individually, and impossible collectively. On the Nahanni, Parks Canada believed it necessary to build a long boardwalk around Virginia Falls to prevent the portage from eroding and becoming a series of gouged creeks—and only 500 canoeists were using the Park. Nevertheless, sensitivity increased. Female canoeists grew in number and, from the beginning of their involvement, they were generally more passive and careful about the environment. Also, canoeing organizations, both provincial and national, began to show more environmental concern, while canoeists as individuals became more active in lobbying for wilderness preservation. Even John Livingston had to admit that, without the efforts of the recreationists who tripped through wilderness, the wilderness advocates would politically have become ineffective.[21] Canoeists could literally see the effects of acid rain, industrial pollution and overdammed rivers.

Yet other facts remained. Deep wilderness travel is generally linear, and canoeists help consume vast quantities of fuel in planes, cars and trains in returning from their destinations. I am not against this; it just needs restating to remove any sense of purity from us. I see the canoe in all its simple, artistic and functional beauty. Yet I also admire the Beaver aircraft and see it as the most alluring and aesthetically satisfying machine extant. Most of us paddle much of the time in synthetic canoes—ABS, kevlar or fibreglass—even if we psychologically think wood-canvas when we hear the word "canoe." And for purists in Ontario, the Maritime-based wood-canvas canoe was itself an impure corruption of the pure cedar-strip. As Mason says, the wood-canvas variety should now "be on the endangered species list."[22] The late 20th century phenomena involving the revival of wilderness canoeing is an elite southern-based, urban-generated one.[23] Many of the canoeists are themselves rather yuppy. Concerned, yes, with preserving a piece of wilderness for their own two-weeks-a-year use, but they are frequently not involved in any examination of their own commitment to urban careerism and to exploitive development. They rarely reflect imaginatively on the cultural significance of the canoe to the Canadian heritage. Often, they seem unconcerned about the need to find new ways for communities in Northern Ontario to have a viable future that is not harmful to the environment and respects the need both for forest conservation and wilderness preservation.

The canoeist should know the ironic role of the canoe in the evolving Canadian culture. The canoe was a serious factor in conflict, death, dichotomy and compromise. Despite the canoe's mythological purity as a symbol, it was, in fact, part of the "idea of progress" which led to the continuing destruction of wilderness and the degradation of the environment.

This ironic truth can give us the knowledge and determination to struggle to preserve parts of that natural environment as seen by the early canoeists in Canada. The canoeist should ultimately know that, in Canadian culture, the myth of the canoe as wilderness symbol is more important than the blurred and complex reality. The canoeist should see that an emotional commitment to the preservation of lands approximating wilderness and a year-round concern for our canoeing heritage is more important than a cold, rational and unreflective control of the canoe on a two-week vacation, away from it all. Usually, the vacation canoe trip is followed by a return to the concrete jungle and to participation in the general degeneration of the Canadian environment, all in the name of economic growth and development. Certainly, the canoeist should avoid and reject the use of expressions connoting conflict with the wilderness. We never "conquer" a river or a route, unless societally, we participate in polluting it or ravaging its shoreline. And then, in the long run, it is we who are conquered. It was perhaps fortuitous that on the new Canadian dollar coin the symbolic voyageur canoe, harbinger of destruction, lost out to the symbolic loon, icon of wilderness. We canoeists should realize we have a special and major responsibility to see that the cry of the loon is never silenced.

Notes

1 *Wilderness Camping*, April-May, 1979.

2 Berton, P. attributed by Dick Brown, *Canadian Magazine*, Dec. 22, 1973, p 3.

3 Hodgins, B. and Hobbs, M. (eds.) *Nastawgan: The Canadian North by Canoe and Snowshoe.* Toronto: Betelgeuse Books, 1985, p 1.

4 Parkin, T. "Add Wings to Your Heels," *Explore*, 32, Sept.-Oct. 1987, p 23.

5 James, W.C. "The Quest Pattern and the Canoe Trip" in Hodgins and Hobbs (eds.) pp 9-23.

6 Mason, B. *Path of the Paddle*. Toronto: Van Nostrand, 1980, p 4.

7 Wadland, J. "Wilderness and Culture" in Hodgins and Hobbs (eds.) pp 223-6.

8 Franks, C.E.S. *The Canoe and White Water: From Essential to Leisure Sport.* Toronto: University of Toronto Press, 1977, pp 53-68.

9 Harris R.C. *The Historic Atlas of Canada, I, From the Beginning to 1800.* Toronto: The University of Toronto Press, 1987, plates 61-3.

10 Pelly, D.F. *Expedition: An Arctic Journey Through History on George Back's River.* Toronto: Betelgeuse Books, 1981.

11 Franks, C.E.S. "David Thompson's Explorations of the Muskoka and Madawaska Rivers" in Hodgins and Hobbs (eds.) pp 25-37.

12 Hodgins, B. "1837: To Temagami by Canoe from near Toronto," *Temagami Times*, January, 1979.

13 Zaslow, M. *Reading the Rocks: The Story of the Geological Survey of Canada, 1842-1972.* Toronto: Macmillan, 1975.

14 Hobbs, M. "Purposeful Wanderers: Late Nineteenth Century Travellers to the Barrens" in Hodgins and Hobbs (eds.) p 81.

15 Morrison, W. *Showing the Flag: The Mounted Police and Canadian Sovereignty in the North 1894-1925.* Vancouver: University of British Columbia Press, 1985.

16 Turner-Davis, T. "Bell, Low, Borron and Paradis: Attitudes Toward the Land, the Native Peoples, and the Future of the James Bay Region." Unpublished paper, Trent University, 1974.

17 *Report of the Survey and Exploration of Northern Ontario, 1900*. Toronto: Government of Ontario, 1901.

18 Hodgins, B. and Benidickson, J. "Resource Management Conflict in the Temagami Forest, 1898-1914," *Historical Papers, 1978*. Ottawa: Canadian Historical Association, 1979

19 Jones, J. *Camping and Canoeing*. Toronto: Briggs, 1903.

20 Livingston, J. *One Cosmic Instant*. Toronto: McClelland and Stewart, 1973; and *The Fallacy of Wildlife Conservation*. Toronto: McClelland and Stewart, 1981.

21 Lingston, J. Speech to the Algonquin Wildlands League, Spring, 1975.

22 Mason, B. p 8.

23 Scanlan, L. "The Fight for the Lady Evelyn," *The Whig-Standard Magazine*, August 15, 1987.

Canoe Sport in Canada: Anglo-American Hybrid?

C. Fred Johnston

Although canoeing in contemporary Canadian society is a multi-faceted activity, canoe images in the Canadian mind are restricted by association with our wilderness environment and history. Images of native craft are fortified by the freighter canoes of explorers and traders. But Canadians also use canoes to sprint short distances, to agonize over marathon distances and to manoeuver deftly through slalom gates suspended over white water. These activities, all associated with competition, are called "sport canoeing."

During the 19th century, British North America was transformed from colonial status to a nation state. Economic and industrial forces accompanied the political transformation, and one outcome was the emergence of a more numerous middle class which demanded more leisure time activities. Canoe sport was one product of this 19th century transformation.

Although native peoples evolved a myriad of canoe-like craft constructed from indigenous materials to serve in hunting, fishing, transportation, commerce and war, they also experimented with contests of speed and canoe skill. Europeans who came here as explorers and fur traders were quick to adopt the aboriginal craft. As they slowly pushed back the wilderness and drew the map of Canada, the long, open stretches of flat water gave prime opportunities for speed play between canoes. Such contests were fought especially keenly when fur trading rivals vied for first access to a portage route. The intermittent tests of endurance and speed added a welcome measure of excitement to an otherwise monotonous activity.

With the merger of the North West and Hudson's Bay Companies in 1821, came an end to the fur trade travel from

Montreal to the North West. The Montreal canoe disappeared from central Canadian waters and the Northern type was relegated to the frontier regions of the country where it was used into the 20th century. Smaller bark craft continued to be used on the fringes of settlement and in the Canadian wilderness. But the craft of the aboriginal peoples, whether it was of bark or log or skin, was not considered suitable for "civilized man." The 19th century sports person was slow to appreciate the legacy of the native peoples.

In the annals of the British contribution to canoe sport no event stands out more significantly as the publication of the slim volume entitled *A Thousand Miles in the Rob Roy Canoe on the Lakes and Rivers of Europe* by the adventurous Scottish barrister, John MacGregor.[1] The book was the product of an enterprising trip through lakes and rivers of Europe in 1865 in a 15-foot kayak-like craft. Constructed clinker style with oak planks and a cedar deck, and weighing an onerous 90 pounds, including lug and jib sails, mast and double-bladed paddle, the first Rob Roy was hardly designed to be hefted on one's shoulders and carried over a portage.

A description of the gear carried by MacGregor illustrates the nature of the canoeing that he popularized. The list included:

Basket to sit on; nails, screws, putty, gimlet, cord, thread, string; buttons, needles, pins, luggage-bag; flannel jacket and two pair of flannel trousers, two flannel shirts, one on the person, the other for the shore; thin alpaca Sunday coat, thin waistcoat; pair of light-sole shoes, straw-hat, two collars, three pocket handkerchiefs; brush, comb, tooth-brush; Testament, tracts for distribution; purse, circular notes and small change; blue spectacles, book for journal and sketches, pen and pencils, maps, cutting off a six inch square at a time for pocket-reference; pipe, tobacco case, and light-box; guide books and pleasant book for evening reading, tear off covers, advertisements, and pages as read, for no needless weight should be carried hundreds of miles—even a fly setting on the boat must be refused a free passage; box of "Gregory's Mixture," sticking plaster, small knife and pencil. Canoe, paddle, mast, sail and luggage, will all weigh about 120 pounds.[2]

Boats, trains and carts were all used to convey the Rob Roy. Frequent inn stops for food and lodging replenished the spirits of the weary paddler. Seven trips and four books established the foundations for MacGregor's literary contribution to the development of canoe sport.

The venturous Scot and his Rob Roy canoe became famous throughout the English-speaking world where gentlemen read the proper magazines such as *The Field* from Britain and *Forest and Stream* from the United States. Canoeing, as popularized by MacGregor, captured the imagination of middle-class gentlemen and influenced the competitive boating events which were already gaining popularity on the Thames River. The earlier appearance of the canoe, as a novelty, accompanied this general interest in boating. Nevertheless to MacGregor must go the credit for building on the youthful canoeing tradition and publicizing its appearance to adventure-hungry, sports-minded people.

But MacGregor's contribution to canoe sport goes beyond the role of publicist. In July of 1866, he organized a canoe club which became the Royal Canoe Club in 1873. Endowed with royal approval, canoeing expanded rapidly, and more clubs were formed throughout Great Britain. The Royal Canoe Club set the annual agenda for the other clubs. Touring was the most popular of club activities, however, and in 1867 the first competition was held, involving 15 canoes. The racing boats were decked canoes propelled by double-bladed paddles and, if the proper water and wind conditions prevailed, with sails. But the competitions were not taken too seriously; they were considered to be gentlemanly games rather than serious competitive sport.

The races hosted by the British Nautilus Canoe Club in 1872 incorporated three canoe classes: paddling (with double blade) in single strake canoes;[3] sailing in first class canoes; and travelling matches. With the introduction of competitions, the British inaugurated the great debate over the relative merits of the different types of craft, a debate that was to consume considerable paper and the idle hours of winter for many an avid canoeist on both sides of the Atlantic.

British plans for the new sport were not confined to the British Isles. In 1869, an abortive effort was made by the Canoe Club to host an invitational race to determine a canoe champion of the World. Invitations were sent to French, US and Canadian canoeists to participate in a two-mile event to be held near Hampton Court on the Thames on the occasion of the four-oared, Oxford-Harvard boat race.

By the mid 1870s the future course of canoeing in Britain was firmly set. The sport was established in the mind of a literary public, thanks to MacGregor's writings and to the public press. Innovative canoe designs emerged to stimulate canoe cruising and racing in both paddling and sailing canoes. The club structure was established and would be copied by sportsmen throughout the world. And the first initiative at international competition was taken. By the late 1870s, British sport canoeing was well established.

In the wilderness areas of Canada, the bark canoes and dugouts of the Indians were readily adopted by gentlemen hunters and fishermen. But they were not accepted as a civilized craft worthy of competitive, middle-class sportsmen. Even more unthinkable was the idea that a gentleman would compete in the same race against an Indian! Such cultural and social prejudices did much to retard the development of canoe sport in Canada's population centres for the first three quarters of the 19th century.

The sport of rowing preceded canoeing in Canada for two reasons. It was an activity well established in the culture of the British who came to Canada. Imperial forces stationed in Canada did much to cultivate competitive sports and aquatic sports, in particular, about the waterside communities of Halifax, Montreal, Kingston, Toronto and Victoria. Rowing dominated aquatics in the early years of the 19th century and, while canoeing was never far removed from these first regattas, local traditions did much to determine the relationship between the two activities.

The first recorded regatta in Halifax Harbour took place in 1826 on the occasion of the visit of his Excellency, the Earl of Dalhousie, Governor General of Upper and Lower Canada. But the lack-lustre appeal of the slow-moving cutter races with crews drawn from the British ships in harbour was in stark contrast to the enthusiastic response which attended the canoe races staged by the local Micmac Indians. In the regattas during the 1830s, the Indian races dominated the festivities and their popularity might account for the trend to more small boat races—gigs, wherries, flats and jolly boats. This in turn prompted the change in the regatta site in 1846 from the unpredictable waters of Halifax Harbour to the smooth waters of Banook Lake on the Dartmouth side of the harbour.

Credit for the founding of the first canoe club in North America, the Chebucto Canoe Club, must go to the British officers stationed at Halifax in the late 1860s. When it was formed is not known, but it was in operation in 1869 when the Canoe Club in England extended the invitation to compete for the World Canoe Championships. Like the mother club in England, the Chebucto Club was a cruising club and the boats used were birch bark or perhaps decked canoes from England.

Lacking an Indian settlement in the vicinity, aquatic sports in the community of Toronto were dominated by rowing and yachting. The first recorded regatta, organized in 1839 by the men of the 32nd Regiment, included rowing events only. Despite almost continuous activity, a paddling race did not appear in the program of the Toronto Rowing Club regatta until 1872. The appearance of canoe races in the Toronto area in the 1870s can be accounted for by the emergence of a new type of craft, the "modern" Canadian canoe.

Canoeing was a common sight about Montreal, going back to the days when Lachine, located above the rapids of the same name, was the embarkation point for the brigades of the North West Company. The merger of the two major fur trade companies in 1821 soon led to the demise of Lachine's role as the eastern terminus of the transcontinental canoe route. But the canoeing traditions were sustained by the Iroquois voyageurs who lived on the reserves of Caughnawaga, across the St. Lawrence from Montreal, and the Lake of Two Mountains, just west of Montreal. The skills of the Indian canoeists were applied in the water transportation industry about Montreal and in the lumbering industry to the north. When the Governor of the Hudson's Bay Company hosted the Prince of Wales' visit in 1860, he organized an impressive canoe pageant off Lachine, and he had no difficulty manning the large Montreal-style canoes with voyageurs from the local reserves.[4]

There were informal rowing races about Montreal before the appearance of the first club in 1864.[5] In the second regatta of the Lachine Boating Club, it was a "war canoe" race staged by the Caughnawagas that captured the attention of the crowd. The canoes used in these races were 30- to 36-feet long and were either log canoes or board canoes constructed clinker style. The annual regattas at Lachine were copiously written up in the Montreal papers and attracted the social elite of Montreal to the shores of Lake St. Louis in subsequent summers. Modern canoe racing appeared on the Montreal scene at the Longueuil Boating Club Regatta in 1875, and at the Grand Trunk Boating Club regatta in 1877.

The appearance of canoe races for gentlemen in the 1870s was associated with the appearance of a different kind of canoe, a wooden canoe built along the lines of the traditional birch bark. This was another so-called "civilized" canoe, but different from that which appeared in Britain.

It was in the backwoods region of Ontario, in the Otonabee valley, where frontier life necessitated a more cooperative, dependent society, that the Indian concept of canoe was subjected to the industrial technology of European culture, and the product was the modern, open, Canadian canoe.

British settlers moved into the valley of the Otonabee in the early 1820s. Isolated and dependent upon the river as highway, settlers had a choice of three different craft: a bark canoe made by the local Mississauga Indians; a log dugout used by both Indians and settlers; and, finally, a plank canoe. Susanna Moodie in her book, *Roughing it in the Bush,* reported the purchase in 1834 of a very light cedar canoe to which she and her husband attached a keel and sail.

The emergence of canoeing competitions along the Otonabee River had a stimulating effect on the search for a more serviceable modern canoe. The Peterborough area had more than its share of British, middle-class families and half-pay officers who brought with them a willingness to work hard but also a tradition for recreation nurtured in the military as well as in the public schools of Britain. During an 1846 regatta on Rice Lake, skiff and sailing races were interrupted for the first organized bark canoe race, added to the program for the local Indians. By 1848 a log canoe replaced the birch bark, and gentlemen sportsmen joined the Indians in the annual canoe races. In the next ten years, the "hog trough" canoe, a phrase popularized by Samuel Strickland, was transformed into an elegant racing machine. By 1861 it, too, was driven from the water by a new and improved wood canoe, the carvel-constructed, basswood, plank, rib and batten canoe. Such canoes were turned out on uniform moulds in assembly line fashion from the shops of John Stephenson, Thomas Gordon and Daniel Herald. This was the type of canoe which found its way to the waterfronts of

Dartmouth, Halifax, Montreal, Toronto and a host of other waterfront settings throughout Eastern Canada in the 1870s.

A meeting of canoeists at Lake George in the Adirondack Mountains of Upper New York state in the summer of 1880 signalled the formation of the American Canoe Association, an organization which was to have a stimulating effect on organized canoeing in the United States, Canada and even Great Britain.

"The Call" for the Canoe Congress, endorsed by twenty-four canoeing enthusiasts largely from the northeastern US, was sent out under Nathaniel Holmes Bishop's hand. A man of independent means who resided at Caldwell on Lake George, Bishop was the focal point of a fellowship of canoe enthusiasts, a position he had earned through his publications.[6]

But the successful transplant of modern canoeing to the US must be shared with William L. Alden, an editorial writer for the *The New York Times* and, later, Consul General to Rome. According to the *Field and Stream* magazine, it was Alden who:

...introduced canoeing into this country, founded the N.Y.C.C. (New York Canoe Club), built the first "Nautilus" ever built on this side of the Atlantic, designed the "Shadow" and made more canoe trips than any other American.[7]

William P. Stephens who chronicled the history of American Yachting in the US, places Alden and canoeing in the context of the times:

Unless he was prepared to go into something large enough to be called a yacht, there were few craft available in those days for the man whose instincts led him to the water. Outside of practice boats and racing shells, there was on the one hand the New York type of centerboard catboat, the worst of the entire breed of "cats," and on the other the 16-foot open Whitehall boat of the Battery boatmen with its small sprit sail. Mr. Alden tried the Whitehall boat on his first cruise up the Hudson; but, as it proved in every way unsuitable, he turned his attention to the Rob Roy canoe, then so popular in England through the cruises and writings of Captain John MacGregor.[8]

The Congress at Lake George in 1880 was intended to bond newly formed local clubs together and to provide the opportunity to contest the canoe skills that had emerged in the isolated regions of the north east. But somewhere between "The

Call" and the publication of the constitution in 1881, the plan for a national association gave way to an "American" association which was meant to include the vast territory of Canada.

The invitation which went out to individuals to join the ACA in 1881 clearly defined its social and sporting biases. An invitation was extended to "all persons of respectable character, of any age, who possessed a true love of nature, and are in earnest sympathy with the brotherhood of cruising canoeists."[9] The races to be held later the same year were to be "innocent competitions between members for prizes contributed by friends and members of the Association. All members being strictly amateurs, professionals will not be admitted to membership, as the Association is not a sporting club..."[10] And it was taken for granted that membership was associated with the ownership of a canoe—one man, one canoe. Or at least that was the vision in the beginning.

Two Canadians heeded "The Call" and journeyed to Lake George in 1880. Robert W. Baldwin, an employee of the Federal Government in Ottawa, made the trip from Ottawa to Lake George in a Rob Roy recently purchased from the Governor General, Lord Dufferin. Representing the "Canadian School" was a hunting and fishing guide from Rice Lake, Thomas Henry Wallace, who turned out to be an oddity with his open Canadian canoe constructed by Herald of Rice Lake. Because canoes were classified for racing according to the primary design features—canoes which could be sailed, sailed and paddled, paddled or paddled and sailed—Wallace, with an open canoe propelled with a single-bladed paddle, had difficulty fitting into the racing schedule. He was allowed to enter two races; the paddling race for Rob Roys and an open-class paddling race. To the surprise of the whole camp, Wallace won both races and carried off one of the choice prizes of the regatta, a Rushton-built Rob Roy canoe.

For the following year the perplexing issue of the open Canadian canoe was resolved by breaking down the paddling canoes into two classes, decked and open. But that was not the end of the classification problems. As the literature so amply demonstrates, the first two decades of the ACA were consumed with the search for the perfect all-purpose canoe.

Canadians responded enthusiastically to the ACA. The first membership from Canada was that of Elihu Burril

Edwards, a Peterborough barrister who became member number 5. The second Canadian, member 67, was Robert Tyson, an avid canoe sailor from Toronto, and a prime mover in the formation of the Toronto Canoe Club in 1880.

At the 1881 meet, the Canadian delegation from Ottawa, Toronto and Peterborough represented a substantial bloc of the 50 paddlers in camp. The reporter for *The New York Times*, observing the arrival of the Peterborough representatives, commented on the Canadian canoes:

...wholly different from ours and carry no sail. They are propelled entirely by the paddles, and the paddle has only a single blade, instead of a double one, as the Americans have...Their boats are the perfection of strength in canoe building; but our American canoeists want a boat to sail and one they can live in when on a long cruise.[11]

The Canadians fared well at Lake George that year. Predictably, they won the Open canoe race, and E.B. Edwards was elected Vice-Commodore. With the 1882 meet, again held at Lake George, the decision was made to move the annual meeting around to other sites to allow local members to participate. With that decision it was only proper that the meet in 1883 should go to Peterborough, to the "true wilderness" of Ontario, and to the home of the first Canadian-born Commodore of the ACA.

Organized canoeing thrived in Canada during the 1880s and 90s virtually from coast to coast, and there emerged a host of clubs, only a fraction of which joined the ACA. The meet of 1883 at Stoney Lake, north of Peterborough, was particularly successful in stimulating the formation of Canadian clubs, especially in Ontario. By 1889 there were 23 Canadian clubs in the ACA.

With a similar response in the US, such speedy growth placed considerable stress on the fledgling organization. For the time being it was saved from internal fracturing with the institution of Divisions, regional associations of member clubs. The Eastern Division of the US was formed in 1886, and the following year the Northern Division, taking in all of Canada, declared itself. Divisional meets, held in close proximity to the region, enabled more paddlers to participate in a summer camp. Such camps took place in Canada at Stoney Lake, Lake of Two Mountains, Pigeon Lake, and Lake Couchiching. Divisional camps expanded membership, but kindled regional solidarities at the expense of the greater association.

At the 1886 meet, the progress of American canoeing was challenged and tested by two visitors from Great Britain, Warrington Baden-Powell and Walter Stewart. Naturally the test was conducted between the foremost canoe sailors. To the satisfaction of the whole camp, Robert W. Gibson and E.H. Barney soundly defeated their British visitors, coming in first and second in two separate races, in part due to the American innovation of the sliding seat. But in the victory there was an element of defeat; the win signalled a triumph for the specialized sailing canoe over the general purpose cruising canoe of the British. The victory widened the gap between canoe sailing and canoe paddling. By 1891 it could be reported that the interest in paddling races was taking precedence over sailing races in the ACA. At the same time it accentuated the differences between the American and Canadian schools of canoeing.

While not fully understood at the time, what was considered a curious innovation at the 1889 camp at Stave Island in the St. Lawrence River, proved in the long run to be a divisive blow to the ACA. The Toronto Canoe Club brought to camp a huge 30-foot club canoe, inappropriately referred to as a "war canoe." Built by the Ontario Canoe Company of Peterborough, the *Unk-Ta-Hee*, "God of the Water," was an imposing sight carrying 16 paddlers, two abreast, each one wielding a single-bladed paddle. The huge, crimson-red, club boat caught the imagination of other clubs in the US and Canada, and five war canoes turned up at the meet at Jessup's Neck, Long Island, the following year. Like a Trojan Horse, the club canoe attacked the one man, one boat principle of membership in the ACA. Throughout the central part of Canada, clubs in Montreal, Ottawa and along the St. Lawrence invested in a boat that was to be owned by the club and not by an individual member. It now became possible to join a club and to paddle without the burden of ownership of a private canoe. The innovation had a democratizing effect on club memberships and it had another more subtle effect: new members to the club were directed to the war canoe where they learned single-blade and not double-blade paddling. Because Canadians were more attracted to the war canoe than their US friends, its introduction further increased the differences between the two schools of canoeing. At virtually any regatta the war canoe race proved to be the most exciting race; club rivalries stimulated training for conditioning and renewed interest in technique and style, any factor which might bring victory.

On April 3, 1900, a meeting of representatives of the Brockville area clubs discussed the formation of a War Canoe League. The action was partly in response to the failure of the ACA to promote war canoe racing to their satisfaction, but it was also instigated by a desire to expand the number of races available to the clubs over the summer. The first meeting led to a second on April 10, at which time a letter was read from E.R. McNeil, Honorary Secretary of the Britannia Boat House Club in Ottawa, which embodied a resolution favouring a regional meeting of clubs to found a War Canoe League. Nine clubs indicated an interest in such an organization, but representatives of six clubs (from Ottawa, Montreal and Brockville) attended the third meeting which took place at the Revere House Hotel in Brockville on May 12. The decision of the meeting was to go beyond the concept of a league to the formation of a national association dedicated to the promotion of all canoe competitions. The new Canadian Canoe Association was not to be considered a rival to the ACA; as the majority of the clubs still wanted to be able to participate in ACA events.

When the first regatta was held at Brockville August 4, 1900, five championship races were held; single-blade singles, tandem, fours and war canoe; and double-blade singles. No canoe sailing events were on the schedule, and the one double-blade race proved unpopular, drawing only two entries. Without regard for theatrics, the program planners commenced the competitions with the war canoe race which did not disappoint the crowd.

Establishment of the CCA in 1900 might be considered as just another minor event on the road to nationhood, but Canadian canoeing's proclamation of independence in North America lacked the language and actions one might associate with a nationalist movement. It appeared to be more of a reaffirmation of some deeply felt legacy that, at the time, could not be articulated. Canoeing in Canada had benefitted from the general sporting stimulus from Great Britain and certainly from the publicity given the sport by the writings of MacGregor. Involvement with the American Canoe Association had stimulated the

growth of canoe sport in Canada at a time when sporting advocates were few and widely dispersed. In the end, canoe sport in
Canada rejected modern canoeing emanating from Great Britain
and the US for a return to its native roots, single-blade paddling
in open Canadian canoes.

Canadian canoeing retained its preference for single-blade
paddling in an open canoe well into the 20th century. Double-
blade paddling was not added to the program of the national
championships until 1932, the consequence of Canadian
involvement in international competition. (In characteristic
fashion, double-blade races took place in open racing canoes.)
Not until the 1950s did the Canadian Canoe Association adopt
the decked racing kayaks used in international canoe racing in
Europe. A stimulus for that decision was the large number of
European paddlers who emigrated to Canada in the years after
the Second World War. Even today, the Canadian preference
for single-blade paddling is reflected in its competition record at
the international level where the majority of our medals have
been won in single-blade singles and tandem events. And it is
a measure of Canada's influence on International sport that the
boats used in single-blade racing are known as "Canadians."
Competitive canoeing is a vibrant part of the Canadian cultural
fabric. It reflects our country's genius for compromise while
staying true to its diverse roots and unique heritage.

Notes

1 MacGregor, J. *A Thousand Miles in the Rob Roy Canoe on the Lakes and
   Rivers of Europe* (7th edition). Boston: Roberts Brothers, 1867.

2 MacGregor, p 2.

3 The single strake canoe took its name from the matched planks of
   Spanish cedar that covered the hull, one plank to each side.

4 *The Tour of H.R.H. The Prince of Wales Through British North America
   and the United States.* Montreal: John Lovell, 1860, p 125.

5 Most sport history literature gives 1863 as the founding date of the
   Lachine Boating Club. The report of the first Lachine regatta (held on
   September 5, 1864) included notice that a club would be formed in the
   community. *Montreal Gazette*, Sept. 5, 1984.

6 Bishop, Nathaniel H. *Voyage of the Paper Canoe.* Boston: Lee and
   Shepard, 1879; and *Four Months in a Sneak Box.* Boston: Lee and
   Shepard, 1879.

7   *Field and Stream*, 9 May, 1878.

8   Stephens, W.P.   *History of the New York Canoe Club.*   Mimeographed abstract from the 1921 50th Anniversary Yearbook of the NYCC, compiled and edited by O.J.   Timberman, p 2.

9   American Canoeing Association, *Constitution.*   Reproduced in Vaux, Boyer.   "History of American Canoeing, Part 2," *Outing Magazine,* 10(4), July 1887, p 363.

10 American Canoeing Association, p 363.

11 *New York Times*, 13 August, 1881.

The Northwest Coast Canoe in Canadian Culture

E.Y. Arima

The phrase "The Canoe in Canadian Culture" sounds perfectly natural, demonstrating how thoroughly Canadian the Algonkian birch bark canoe has become. However, if one says "The Northwest Coast Canoe in Canadian Culture," things are quite different. A skeptic might even ask, "But is the Northwest Coast canoe really in Canadian culture?" I say yes, but barely.

It can be confidently stated that the Northwest Coast dugout canoe is often a superlative one, greatly admired for its beauty, fine lines, and excellent performance characteristics. It is a craft which *ought* to be a much cherished element in Canadian culture. This suggestion reflects the fact that the Northwest Coast canoe is no longer the common sight on our Pacific waters that it was even well into this century. In fact, there were several different craft that fell into this category of canoe.

The phrase "Northwest Coast" came into use only after English-speaking explorers and traders came to the region for sea otter pelts in the 18th century (i.e. after James Cook's visit to Nootka Sound in 1778). The term delimits the area:

From Puget Sound in Washington Territory to Mount St. Elias in southern Alaska, the coast line is broken into a continuous archipelago. The Cascade Mountains, running throughout this territory parallel to the coast line, leave, adjacent to the Pacific, a strip of country about 150 miles broad and 1,000 miles long, called generally The North West Coast.[1]

There is a cultural continuity in the whole area, extending even farther south into northern California on cultural grounds, reflecting a certain environmental constancy: the Black Current

flowing northward from the tropics moderates the climate and
loads the prevailing westerly with moisture which condenses
into heavy coastal precipitation. The temperate rain forest
which results has huge trees, including the red cedar which is
especially good for canoes. As dense undergrowth made land
movement difficult, people travelled mostly by water. It is said
that so customary was it to go by canoe, a man would embark
just to visit a friend down the beach.

In choosing living sites, having a beach for landing and
launching a canoe was an important consideration. So much
were people in canoes that their very physique appeared affected, with the upper body well developed at the expense of the
lower. A description of paddling position helps one understand
this phenomenon:

In the smaller canoes one knelt or sat on the bottom. The usual
posture was the kneeling one in which the paddler rested his weight
on his feet which he turned sideways, heels outward. This position
becomes very uncomfortable to one not accustomed to it, but the
Nootkans were inured to it from childhood. It undoubtedly accounts
for the rather clumsy, pigeon-toed stiff-ankled gait of the older people, as many of the early explorers suggested. Paddlers in the big
canoes either sat on the thwarts or stood.[2]

The Northwest Coasters were Canada's canoe people *par
excellence.* They lived principally on the rich food resources of
the North Pacific: salmon, halibut, herring, cod, seals, sea lions,
porpoises, whales, shellfish and other invertebrates. With
supplementary land animals and plants, they enjoyed a food
surplus, a rare situation for hunters and gatherers, and were
able to support time-consuming, not immediately productive
activities like dugout canoe carving spread over several weeks
or months. People were generally sedentary for long periods,
especially in the big winter villages, though there were seasonal
moves made by canoes. They were sometimes linked into
catamarans with a bridging platform of planks which was home
for weeks. Large social groups existed with a strong concern for
rank based on heredity and wealth. There were Chiefs who had
to have ostentatious big canoes. Wars occurred, fostering special
war canoes. Such solid economic and social reasons lie behind
the existence of the highly developed Northwest Coast dugout
canoes. Yet at the same time the designs seem to have a life of

their own, appearing to have grown as much in accordance with water conditions and canoe-maker traditions.

While there are several different classifications of Northwest Coast canoes, about a dozen major varieties can be recognized, not counting those class distinctions that seem to be made mostly on the basis of size differences. These major varieties can be combined into three general types: Northern or Haida style canoes; Southern or Nootka, sometimes called Chinook canoes; and River canoes.[3] The Coast Salish canoes of the Straits of Georgia and Juan de Fuca and of Puget Sound could be a fourth distinct category, or a low-sided variant of the Northern style.

The major canoe traditions or styles, their forms, performance characteristics, tribal and historical associations all have a bearing on their interrelationship with Canadian culture. Comparative studies of Northwest Coast canoes are relatively few but the work of Durham[4] and of Roberts and Shackleton[5] are particularly useful.

The Haida canoe had characteristically high projecting ends. The stem had a vertical edged cutwater blade, while the stern rose uninterrupted from the bottom in a grand sweep upward, often to an even greater height than the stem. Some canoes were built quite angularly with rather straight bottom lines to the end projections and the bottom itself, while others were shaped more curvaceously. Some looked boxy and bulky, others more slender and graceful. Builders obviously shaped the hull carefully for certain degrees of tracking, turning ability, balance fore and aft, and the like. Inside, there were thwarts set lower than in Southern canoes. Sometimes, in fancy large canoes, shaped seats were carved into the thwarts near the sides for better paddling. Canoes were often painted decoratively outside on the end quarters, the main body amidships usually remaining plain black. The inside could be solid red or white. Carved wooden sculptures could be put on the ends, added on top or as relief pieces on the sides, for ceremonial occasions.

Besides a small, undecorated hunting version of the Haida canoe, there existed family or transportation canoes, 25 to 35 feet long and 4 to 6 feet in beam, that could carry 2 tons or more of people and gear. There were also long-distance voyaging canoes, 35 to 65 feet long and 6 to 8 feet in beam, traditionally with painted designs and sometimes carving at the ends.

To the north, the Yakutat canoe was almost evenly curved along its whole length. The hull was rounded and full-bodied, giving these small craft considerable capacity for their length. The most distinctive detail was the triangular fin at either end. The one at the bow usually projected farther forward than the prow; the after fin was made vertical, a few inches inboard from the end. Indian rationalization for these appendages was that the bow spur fended off ice, protecting the hull, and the long waterline made the canoe easier to hold on course. Two-person Yakutat canoes were as small as 15 feet long by 2 feet broad, and weighed only 80 pounds. The four-person size was 18 feet in length and 3 feet in beam.

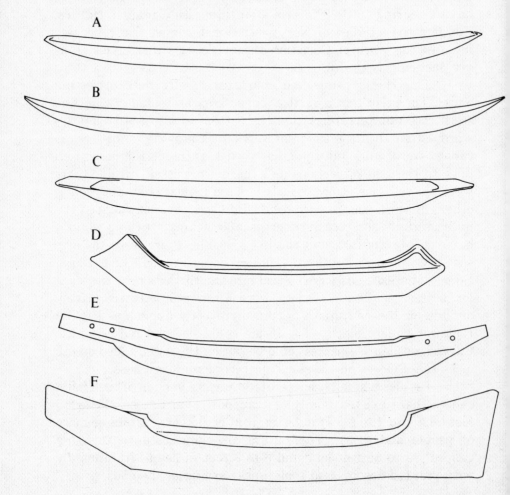

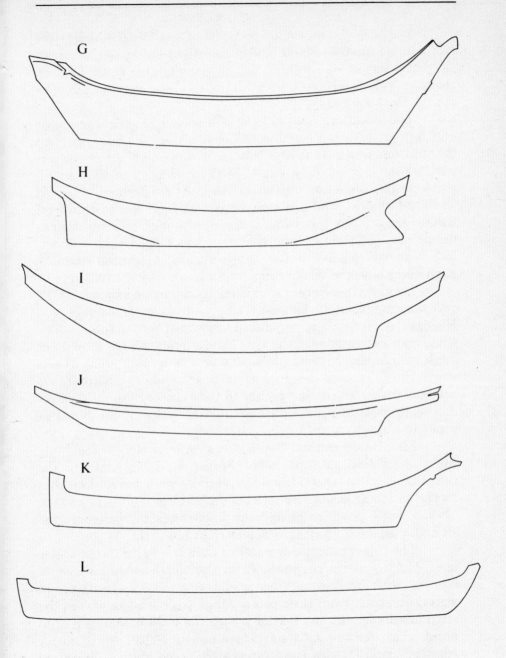

Figure 1.   Outlines of Northwest Coast Canoes: (Not to Scale) A—Shovelnose; B—Spoon; C—Punt-form; D— Yurok; E—Tlingit; F—Haida; G—Kwakiutl menka; H—Yakutat Tlingit; I—Haida; J—Coast Salish; K—Nootka; L—Nootka derivative, Quinault.

The idiosyncratic notched prow of the small Yakutat design calls to mind the bifid bow of the Aleut baidarka, especially since this kayak was well known to the Tlingits, being used by them at Yakutat Bay. The model is of a size very suitable for recreational use today.

The Southern, Nootka, or Chinook canoe is the major alternative sea-going Northwest Coast canoe. Its bow rises but not quite as much as in the Northern canoe, while the stern is vertical or just slightly raked with a characteristic small, platform-like elevation on top. Both ends are formed by added on "head" pieces, and are scooped out at the sides to throw off waves. Decoration was usually spare, although painted designs did occur. Most noticeably, the stem was tipped with a snout-like form which gave it the appearance of a stylized animal's head and made the whole canoe seem like a living creature.

Local style differences existed, as might be expected. The two leading Nootkan canoe-making centres of Clayoquot and Nitinat, for instance, produced constrasting shapes.   The Clayoquot cutwater met the bow head's leading edge at a slight angle, while the Nitinat prow was one smooth curve. At the stern, the Clayoquot design was vertical, while the Nitinat was raked a little. Such fine points to us were obvious to natives, and awareness of them will enhance the place of the Nootkan canoe in Canadian culture.

Like Haida canoes, Nootka boats were widely traded, into the Gulf of Georgia, the lower Fraser, and far south to the Columbia and beyond. Local derivatives were made, like that by the Quinault located 80 miles south of Cape Flattery, and the Makah, both of which lacked the fineness of the original—the stem, for example, having a nondescript blunt tip.

The Coast Salish canoe, other than the River designs they used, has a general resemblance to the Northern canoe in profile, but with substantially lower ends and sides as befits use in waters removed from the open ocean. A mouth-like slot in the stem just under the top border brings the bifid baidarka bow to mind. This feature may have meaning in Salish spirit terms. Another usual feature is an integrally carved, outwardly raised border at the gunwales like a washstrake applied outside, on the inside of which is a scooped-out band for a sponson effect.[6] This was also present in the Yakutat design. There is photographic record of a very fine looking, sleek variety at Nanaimo with a long, slim, overhanging projection at the stern as well as the stem. Although less recognized than the Northern and so-called Southern canoes, the Coast Salish design is also very appealing.

The Haida and Nootka canoes invite comparison. One observer rates the Haida model as "swifter, handier and more buoyant."[7] Another found the Nootka models to be "roomier, drier, sturdier and less crank, bearing that simple perfection which is the higher art."[8] For a positive word on the Coast Salish design, we hear Chief Charles Jones of Port Renfrew on the West Coast of Vancouver Island. A centenarian, he must be the last one alive who went fur sealing in the Bering Sea in a Nootkan canoe. Of his Coast Salish neighbours' craft he says, "They have a very good model, very fast. We can't catch them!"

River canoes may be separated into several varieties, mainly distinguished by their end configurations. The ends are usually bluntly rounded below. Sides are quite parallel, the hull remaining full until near the very ends for a trough-like appearance which is pronounced when the ends are squared off above as on a punt. With the ends rounded off, river canoes have been called "shovel-nose" or "spoon" if they happen to be somewhat pointed. In Canadian territory, spoon canoes are known from the Bella Coola region and shovel-noses from the Fraser River. At the southern end of the Northwest Coast region, the Yurok Indians produced out of redwood, carefully made, distinctive, river canoes with peaked ends. The punt-like and shovel-nose varieties could have a slightly elevated poling platform at one or both ends. River canoes obviously work well in rivers but lack the glamour of the sea designs and may stay rather obscure in Canadian cultural terms.

Northwest Coast canoes are not today as much a part of Canadian culture as the eastern birch bark canoe. The primary reason for the difference must be historical, the birch bark canoe having been a necessary part of the beaver fur trade which to a large degree formed Canada. The birch bark canoe was extensively used by Canadians in the fur trade who became able to make them and even created their own varieties like the large *canot du maître*. On the other hand, the Northwest Coast canoes, although very much involved in the sea otter trade of the late 18th and early 19th century,[9] were never really used by the fur traders who could move everywhere required in sailing ships.

The Northwest Coast natives hunted the sea otter and fur seal from their canoes.   There is no reason that Canadians, Europeans or Americans in the Pacific fur trade could not have built and used Northwest Coast dugout canoes had it been necessary or desirable.   During the 19th century gold rushes, they did use them in substantial numbers for transport up the Fraser to the Cariboo and in Chilkat territory to head for the Klondike.   Also, there was some use by early colonists and government officials in their travels.

But the intensive recreational canoeing in Canadian and American culture, which developed from the birch bark canoe and its derivatives, never materialized for the Northwest Coast designs.   Sailboats became the leading recreational watercraft on west coast waters and motorboats came in for work and re-creation.   The natives themselves preferred sails first and then motors, using both with their canoes.   Today factory-made motorboats are the craft of choice for west coast native people. With the exception of some museum specimens, still workable, dugouts have passed into history.

Canadian culture has not taken up the Northwest Coast canoes in a physically active manner although, in mental symbolic ways, it has not entirely forgotten them.   Like a num-ber of other eye-catching native items, Northwest Coast canoes contribute to a distinctive Canadian identity.   By good fortune, the two most accomplished canoe carving peoples, the Haida and Nootka, happen to be within Canada's national boundaries, as are the builders of the pleasing Coast Salish design.   Increasing awareness of them can only improve chances of their more active incorporation into modern Canadian culture.

Culture has been defined, in a phrase, as "life experience." It also entails inherited group traditions and a de-gree of coherent integration with patterning or style.[10] Three main cultural realms are commonly distinguished as the mate-rial, mental and social.   Canoes belong fundamentally to the material cultural sphere, of course, though they have aspects of the other realms as well.

Another anthropological approach says cultural items have four salient aspects: form, use, meaning and function in the sense of perpetuation of the culture,[11] and that in cross cultural transfer—as is involved in relating Northwest Coast canoes to Canadian culture—form takes precedence over the other qualities and influences their development in the new setting. The qualities can and will change from the original, including form, but the initial form is important since it strongly influences what uses, meanings and functions will become associated with the item after transfer.

In Northwest Coast canoes, their form can appear so distinctive, so native, that it might inhibit Canadians in general from using them, despite their practicality in terms of physical performance. Their highly idiosyncratic appearance may also deter the development of new meanings in Canadian cultural terms. On the other side of the fence, the distinctness of form of the canoes provides a strong focal point for native identity as the occasional reconstructions made in the present period demonstrate.

The direct and effective way to increase the presence of Northwest Coast canoes in Canadian culture today is to make and use them as recreational watercraft. After the general demise of the original dugout canoes as working boats, some people have been doing just that in the second half of this century. There are the native canoe makers who kept their craft going in places like Kitimat and Nitinat. The Coast Salish maintained continuity in building racing canoes. Where tradition has been broken, revivalists have arisen: the Tate brothers, among the Tsimshian; the Williams of Clayoquot; and the Haida artist Bill Reid, together with Gary Edenshaw. There are also non-native makers and users who are important because they take the Northwest Coast forms fully into the broader national culture.

There have also been Northwest Coast forms made in non-traditional materials and ways which are of interest since they may indicate the direction of future, larger scale production. In an issue of *Alaska White Water* magazine of the early 1960s, there was an advertisement for native watercraft designs in fibreglass which showed a Nootkan canoe as well as a 25-foot East Canadian Arctic kayak. More recently, Phil Nuytten in Vancouver has produced a fibreglass Northern style canoe which, although too boxy in the hull and wide in the end projections, is excellently crafted and incorporates computerized analysis. A couple of northern style canoes are being used by modern Kwakiutl, mainly for recreation. Another recent instance of non-traditional construction and modified form is a little 14-foot Nootka type, designed and built by John Marples for the Makahs at Neah Bay, using Jim Brown's constant camber construction techniques.[12] There are plans to build the canoe in series for export to Japan. Modernization of the Northwest Coast designs seems to be underway.

For individuals to take the lead in making and using the traditional forms, or derivatives, information and images are vital. With these, there is a good chance for increased presence and enjoyment of the Northwest Coast styles in Canadian culture.

Notes

1   Niblack, A.P. *The Coast Indians of South Alaska and Northern British Columbia.* Washington: United States National Museum Annual Report, 1890, p 231.

2   Drucker, P. *Indians of the Northwest Coast.* New York: Natural History Press, 1955.

3   These categories come from the work of Olson, R. *Adze, Canoe, and House Types of the Northwest Coast.* Washington: University of Washington Publications in Anthropology 2(1), 1927, pp 19-21; and from Drucker, pp 72-6.

4   Durham, W. *Indian Canoes of the Northwest Coast.* Seattle: Copper Canoe Press, 1960.

5   Roberts, K.G. and Shackleton P. *The Canoe: A History of the Craft from Panama to the Arctic.* Toronto: Macmillan Press, 1983.

6   Roberts and Shackleton, p 112.

7   Niblack, p 295.

8   Durham, p 48.

9   Cook, W.L. *Flood Tide of Empire: Spain and the Pacific Northwest.* New Haven: Yale University Press, 1973, pp 100-11.

10 Kroeber, A.L. and C. Kluckhohn. "Culture: A Critical Review of Concepts and Definitions," Boston: Harvard University Papers, Peabody Museum of American Archaeology and Ethnology 47(1)c, 1952, p 15.

11 Linton, R. *The Study of Man: An Introduction.* New York: Appleton Century, 1936, p 16.

12 O'Brien, M. "Launchings," *Wooden Boat* 78, 1987, pp 96-8.

Reflections of
a Bannock Baker

Bob Henderson

Recently, I visited an office tower in downtown Ottawa. A friend was showing me the view of the Peace Tower, the Chateau Laurier, and the National Gallery to the north. While he was pointing these out, I noticed the hills of the Gatineau in the distant misty haze. Best of all, I saw with excitement the Gatineau River cutting into the hills, its mouth flowing into the Ottawa River. I imagined myself in a canoe at the head of this valley. I thought of it as an ancient, native trade route. I thought of the other rivers that flow from the north into the Ottawa—ones I've paddled and ones I haven't. I thought of the Canadian Shield generally, and the magic in the partnership of landscape, canoe and paddler. I thought of myself as a paddler, seeking out this genius.

Then I clicked back into being courteous and receptive to my penthouse office guide, and I was looking at the stodgy parliament buildings, hotels, and museums. I dared not share my wandering thoughts at the time, for fear of appearing a hopeless romantic. I remained quietly detached. I felt out of joint, as we turned away, wondering whether I was stuck in the past or strangely ahead of my time.

So exists a secret vision of place and time—private island of thoughts in rushing traffic. Despite living most of my life in cities, my life's force seems to focus on the canoe and its landscape. My deepest desires are to be a part of this partnership and my greatest despair is the keen difficulty of the relationship.

In addressing the topic of the canoe and Canadian culture, I must be personal and emotional. I'll explain why my eye was drawn to the Gatineau Valley and not the cityscape on that August morning. I'll explain my title. In short, I propose to express my personal relationship to the canoe and the way it helps to evolve an understanding of Canadian culture. I need not fear appearing egotistical and self-indulgent by overly romanticizing my relationship to the canoe because, if I comprehend the idea of nexus correctly, I assume we are of like minds and my story will resonate with your own.

The relationships linking canoe, terrain and culture are powerful but difficult. They are intangible and appreciated beyond one's head and hands. The power draws me to focus gaze and thought on a distant river valley in preference to towering buildings. To head and hands is added heart. The difficulty lies in the incompleteness of the relationship, to bring heart into play as an equal, as a glue. I'm so trapped in my civilized skin that my synchrony with the canoe always feels less than it could be. But the spirit here is one of quests, not absolutes, as we seek the essence of relationship. We wish to find the heart of the wilderness travel experience and develop a mindscape focused on love for a craft and geography; the relationships that always remain a challenge; the natural world and our role in it.

How do we enter into this special but difficult relationship among canoe, landscape and culture? For many Canadians the process begins in their earliest years. My childhood memories include the bear snacking on our peanut butter and jam on Tanamakoon Lake, and crying on the 900 yard portage between Smoke and Kootchie Lakes. I remember the wind preventing me from reaching my goal in Wigwam Bay while singling a canoe. I was seven. It was my first summer at camp. I recall my excitement when driving up to summer camp each year, and the completion of this excitement satisfied by the act of etching the summer's canoe routes on the family map of Algonquin Park tucked into an attic corner on the wall with a chest below it so I could sit close.

Over the years I etched with pride many of the possible Algonquin routes on our busy map. I was a young river-bagger. By the time I was sixteen, my summer canoe trips were the most important thing in my life. When, as a senior camper, I first saw native pictographs in Quetico Provincial Park, my fate was sealed. There were new maps to etch, not only with routes, but with heritage locations as well. After that trip in Quetico, I discovered the library. I found Sigurd Olson's *The Lonely Land*, and my delight in reading for pleasure began. I had been labelled dyslexic in grade six and, up to that point, I was "not a reader."

With an opportunity to lead a trip in Quetico, a new habit of research became linked to the process of canoeing. I became a studious reader. I studied the geology, history, place names, pictographs—anything I could find. But guiding trips provided another interest—teaching and interpretation. The guiding, the marking of maps, and the exploration of libraries led without much planning to graduate school and to a private ambition to become the consummate Canadian wilderness guide.

It has been said that "subjects exist only in schools." Real learning is a personal, totally engaging process, driven by a burning curiosity. There, the limitations of partial thinking are lost. During these years I discovered that there are no fields of study on a river, no specialists establishing fame and security by escaping the whole. Eventually, the river runs free to the open seas, but it starts with rivulets and streams connecting like larger understandings, gathering and growing. So it is that the canoe can be the starting point, travelling from the branches, and building an endless study of humanity, nature, and relationship.

Canoe travel can provide a forum for such broadly based learning—an engaging nexus which intertwines a wide spectrum of academic disciplines. What I know about the humanities and the natural and social sciences, is all due to a single curiosity in relationship—the canoe. Each bit of learning leads to another, furthering new inquiry, understanding and applications. The wise eclectic is both branching out and gathering in at the same time.

My first official title was Head of Canoe Tripping for the school I attended (which I attended of course because it had canoe tripping). My university efforts were channelled from the canoe as a centre-piece. I managed to write canoe-related assignments for courses in Historical Geography, Sociology of Sport, Anthropology, English, Kinesiology, and more. But I was no specialist in my eyes. I was just pursuing interests, branching out and gathering in.

Today, this starting-point curiosity is hardly spent. It is still taking shape. In fact, now I regret the missed opportunities I had during early school years for canoe-related projects when I could not think up an angle to link my interests to course content. I got comically efficient at this by graduate school, and happily now do not face many barriers.

There is no prospect of boredom or repetition with this apparently narrow focus. There is the history of canoe country—native peoples and Euro-Canadians. There are biomechanics for racing, tripping and aesthetic styles. There are natural history, earth science, preservation and conservation struggles. There are cultural values and politics. There is learning how all these are best learned and the excitement of sharing my thoughts and lessons. It wasn't until I tried talking or writing about these ideas that connections grew and matured. All this deserves exploration. So while the river grows from headwater, branches and funnels to the sea—the wide horizon beyond—so, too, is the canoe eclectic, always looking in and looking out, ideally in a happy balance.

What I discover about canoes and myself through canoes is an understanding of Canadian culture. This understanding, albeit romantic, is a healthy one, well graced in heritage appreciations, with a focus on the land now—that most tangible Canada—the Canada worth working for. Strangely enough such learning seems to be gaining momentum in a modern context. Interests that are based in old wisdoms, outdated crafts, materials and designs, are now visible, culturally speaking. Put simply, the canoe and all that goes with it is *in* (but not quite *in* enough for that major office complex). Words like "natural," "ecology" and "preservation" are in greater usage and application. Use of natural materials and traditional designs are in vogue. The world views of aboriginal peoples are in review. Concern for canoeable environments, whether they be Hamilton's harbour, Temagami's reserve, or Queen Charlotte's shoreline, are worthy of debate. Preserving natural integrity and re-establishing a natural look are modern concerns. All that I might have thought would make me a "nerd" back in high school is now making me anything but. Perhaps James Bond will be on a canoe trip in the Canadian Shield, struggling to save a threatened ecosystem, for his next epic adventure.

But, back to reality. There is both a sense of timelessness and tranquility that goes with canoeing. These feelings come from fitting in with history, tapping a connection to Canada's beginnings in the here-and-now and having a concern to preserve the future integrity of this activity. So, past, present and future meet, and I'm made to realize that my education won't make me a twentieth century specialist but a hopeless amateur, faithful to Arne Naess's plea, "seek simplicity to preserve complexity."[1] These ideas emerge most powerfully from reflecting on bannock. Bannock is a form of soda bread. It is flour, baking powder, and water mixed and baked by the radiant heat of the fire. It has a long tradition in the Canadian north woods and remains a hearty staple today for canoe trippers. Although this is quite enough, baking bannock is much more.[1]

Baking bannock on canoe trips is a simple ritualistic expression of a deep basic drive to satisfy hunger. It is an instinctively warm experience because the canoe tripper is linked to every aspect of the product. One has bought quality ingredients, packed them, carried them, and now caringly bakes them over an equally thoughtful fire—soon to eat them. This is an instinctual drive, complete. On the opposite end of the continuum is popping into a burger place, consuming the food, and you're out the door without any thought. This is an instinctively cold experience that leaves one empty in a qualitative way at least.[3]

Baking bannock is an active part of the life process. Grabbing the convenient burger is happening outside us, devoid of relationship and appreciation. There is a philosophical motive for the simple chore of baking bannock on canoe trips. Fulfilling basic needs such as hunger and shelter, the engaging process of baking on a warm fire, perhaps with a few friends quietly absorbing the heat, sustains the body and nurtures friendship. This defies our modern unchallenged rhetoric of progress, and provides a redirection to evaluate our progress. As Australian poet Banjo Paterson (a remarkable counterpart to Robert Service) warns, "for the town folk have no time to grow, they have no time to waste."[4] But bannock isn't the only item on canoe trips where simplicity and relationship applies.

The modern canoe trip, when stripped down to basics, is simply going to different places to eat, looking at the view as you go. Now, that's simple. Bannock is a metaphor for canoe tripping. Canoeing likewise is a ritualistic expression of our Canadian traditions, and we modern, canoe-tripping holidayers are most often struck first by its warm simplicity of lifestyle. This is a lifestyle that engages one's whole being in active relationship. It, too, is a metaphor for how to live. An example of travel in a cold medium is the average airplane journey where the traveller takes it all for granted and is totally detached from the process. "Thinking biologically and psychologically, camp life is more natural; thinking realistically, city life is more natural."[5] The canoe trip teaches many dimensions of the quality of life.

It's simple! Bannock is simple, canoeing is simple, life becomes simple. One understands all the processes and materials around them and becomes fully engaged in the environment. I understand my canoe, the map, fire lighting, my reflector oven. I know how they work, what they are made of, and how this is done. As I sit here in my office, I know very little about what is around me. My office environment leaves me cold and alienated. I am detached from many of the processes around me. My desk is mock wood. The lights are neon. How is this possible? Air is circulating, making a noise. How does this work? Of course, I can learn answers to these questions and all others pertaining to man-made products and man-made environmental conditions. My office environment is not simple but it is easy to figure out and to know that it is cold in terms of a sense of security. On canoe trips, things are simple but difficult to *really* figure out. That is the magic, our gateway to our spiritual self.

I said I understood fire and canoeing, but one's understanding of natural processes will always come to a point where it is incomplete. After that point, it is a mystery—the third thing, as D.H. Lawrence might have said: "Water is hydrogen two parts, oxygen one, but there is also a third thing that makes it water and nobody knows what this is."

I understand the radiant heat of the fire. I thank the sun when the heat it stored in wood warms me. I understand fire requires four elements—heat, fuel, oxygen and uninhibited chain reactions—but I understand this only up to a point. From this point on, nature offers a universal confusion that forces us to ask spiritually enriching questions like Who am I, and How am I linked to all of this? Asking such questions stems from instinctively warm experiences. We should be secure in the unknowns of the natural world; we should feel it as our true sense of place.

This mystery that is beyond one's comprehension, that is common to all the natural world and absent in the man-made products, is the complexity Arne Naess pleads for us all to preserve. It is akin to Thoreau's famous adage, "in wildness is the preservation of the world." Spiritually we need this wildness in self and in nature.

The canoe can serve as one of the gateways to relearn this wisdom—to appreciate the wonder of nature and its rich complexity and to practice a simple, stripped-to-basics lifestyle to preserve a wild complexity. According to Sigurd Olson, "a man is part of his canoe and therefore part of all it knows. The instant he dips a paddle he flows as it flows."[6] The canoe trip is often a Canadian's first exposure to a society which necessarily conserves and attends primarily to life's necessities. A removal from a consumer society shrouded in complicated surroundings, it is within our grasp of comprehension because it is mostly man-made, yet also beyond our present understanding due to the rapid changes of the information explosion. The canoe trip brings us back to basic experiences, like paddling a creek on a misty morning in search of moose, sitting on cool granite and baking bannock. We come to see that, for a true sense of simplicity and complexity, one will actually meet the other. We change in the process. Words like "getting away from it all," are often used to describe this change. I suggest that more accurate terms are "surfacing" and "stimulated." Few fail to feel a sense of release, of stimulation or surfacing, with those first few strokes.

This is the stuff we, of western culture, need. We need to see ourselves as linked to natural process, not in a hierarchical fashion above it all. The simplicity of the canoe trip—of baking bannock—exposes nature's complexity to us. We are humbled by its unknowns. This is the great promise of the canoe.

I doubt I will ever experience the degree of magical affinity with the genius of self and canoe that drives my imagination. Rather, these intangibles, with some direct thought and concrete experience, can be cultivated, the result being enrichment of past life, vision of future life, contentment with present purposes.

Take a look around the planet. I think we humans need to change the way we think and act. The canoe has helped me onto this path, seeking simplicity to preserve complexity. It is a difficult but also rewarding path in these modern times full of hypocritical actions and frustrated thoughts and deeds. It is the joys and frustrations that are the nexus for Canadian paddlers everywhere. Many of these joys are inexpressible, hard-to-grasp feelings that we rarely address but are the essence of experience.

Promising outgrowths of simple canoeing pursuits and a "no fields of study on a river" approach can inspire an experienced sense of place and relatedness in environment, a sense of timelessness and tranquility, a sense of identity, and an absorbing curiosity for exploration. To borrow from D.H. Lawrence's phrasing, the canoe is a watercraft pointed at each end, but there is a third thing that makes it a canoe that is brought into play with human relationship and nobody really knows what it is.

I am not suggesting the canoeist should be the model, a noble savage—that it is only the natural life that is good for him or her—that we should all seek a lost innocence of man in wilderness. This is a facade. We should and must appreciate the significance of the natural, nonhuman relationships in our lives to prevent what Aldo Leopold feared: that "education and culture have become almost synonymous with landlessness."[7] The canoe is the great Canadian way to avoid landlessness. The canoe relationship works to balance a life.

Here I remain, keen to etch more maps and pursue still-waiting waterways, happy with memories and respect for travelled routes. I remain eager to delve into deeper nooks and aisles of libraries and I'm still trying to figure out wise guiding and interpretation strategies, and ways and means to protect the land. Connecting all this is the desire to be a part of, in harmony with, my canoe and whatever the present environment may be. Mostly I want to experience nature, not theorize about it. To learn and to share is the directive that evolved from a focussed passion for canoes, maps, and the Canadian Shield—canoe country. I am still working on that consummate Canadian Canoe Guide idea.

So far, I have learned that there are no fields of study on a river and that baking bannock by the fire in the bush and all that goes with it can work to change one's world view. It can bring one into nature with head, hand, and heart.

Notes

1 Naess, A., as expressed in Kvaløy, S. "Ecophilosophy and Ecopolitics: Thinking and Acting in Response to the Threats of Ecocatastrophe," *North American Review*, Summer, 1974, pp 20-21.

2 I would like to express my thanks to Joss Hablien who taught me the importance of bannock.

3 Elrick, M. "The Only Life Worth Living." Unpublished essay, McMaster University, 1986.

4 Paterson, A.B. "Clancy of the Overflow" in *The Man From Snowy River and Other Verses*. Sydney: Pacific Books, Angus and Robertson Ltd., 1929.

5 Hendy, C.E. and Dimock, M.S. *Camping and Character*. New York: Associated Press, 1929.

6 Olson, S. *The Singing Wilderness*. New York: Alfred A. Knopf, 1956, p 77.

7 Leopold, A. *A Sand County Almanac*. Toronto: Oxford University Press, 1949, (1982 reprint) p 210.

Motives for Mr. Canoehead

Philip Chester

The wilderness to us is more than just an empty place out there, it is part of every Canadian's idea of himself and his ancestry. If not in body, then in his imagination.[1]

When I heard about *Canexus* my first thought was that this must be the working title of Henry Miller's lost manuscript. As a prurient undergraduate I'd read *Nexus*, *Plexus*, and *Sexus*, but *Canexus*? That was a new one. As I soon discovered to my delight, however, *Canexus* would be a conference followed by a book to celebrate the canoe in Canadian culture. It was Pierre Berton, the man who has done more for bow ties than a kilted Farley Mowat has done for the sale of boxer shorts, who once observed that "a Canadian is someone who can make love in a canoe." While this may or may not be true, I would add that, unlike his American cousin, the true Canadian knows enough to take out the centre thwart. Taking out the centre thwart is what this essay is about.

The view from inside an upturned canoe may be absurd, but it belongs to my hero Mr. Canoehead (that martini-time Frantics' caricature on "Saturday Night Live" who became a super hero when his head was inadvertently welded to his aluminum canoe by an errant lightning bolt) who is trying to tell us something about ourselves. We would do well to listen even if he does behave like a half-witted brother straight out of William Faulkner's *The Sound and the Fury*. On this prosaic journey, I hope to portray the canoe itself balancing at the fulcrum point of an emerging Canadian identity which, I believe, this unique collection is attempting to pry out of the Precambrian bedrock of our collective unconscious, presuming, of course, with Carl Jung, that such a mythopoeic creature exists. It is high time we paid tribute to not just an object but a way of life, a way of looking at life. My tale will not be the professor's tale, or the canoe builder's tale, but the unknown writer's tale, written by a man who perceives in the image and form of the canoe the central informing power behind a uniquely Canadian myth. This myth to which Canadians subscribe, rightly or wrongly, has been lying dormant for the better part of four hundred years, and is finally beginning to see the light of day. My purpose in this essay, is to help deliver the overdue baby whose pulse we can feel but which has not yet taken its first breath, even though we have given it a name.

My key reference here is Joseph Campbell's *The Hero with a Thousand Faces*.[2] This book outlines the skeleton of the standard quest as revealed in such ancient myths as the tales of Perseus, Jason, and Prometheus, and in such modern stories as *The Lord of the Rings*, *Moonfleet*, and *Star Wars*. The structure of such narratives is old, but there are two points of note: not all stories of this kind necessarily follow a predetermined formula; and different myths will stress different aspects of the quest, depending on the author.

Northrop Frye's classification of heroes[3] from literature is convenient evidence of the truth in the quest mythology. One finds surprising resonance in Frye's categories of hero:

Super person superior in kind; can defy natural law; can solve problems so grave that mere mortals can no longer cope with them;

Supreme person similar to super person, but appears to be human; seems to defy natural laws; capable of making mistakes;

Leader mortals identify with this person; we can aspire to the leader's qualities of leadership because what he or she represents is (at least theoretically) within our grasp; the best of human qualities that society can produce;

Common hero ordinary person; rises to the occasion and therefore becomes extraordinary;

Lowly person at best inept and at worst disreputable.

But my critical perspective comes not from what can be *found* in our literature about heroes or canoes. Rather, I'm concerned with what *cannot* be found, and hope to suggest reasons why there has never been a major, serious work of fiction ever written in this country about a mode of transportation which has so obviously played a key role in our economic, social and political development.   When Mr. Boswell asked Dr. Johnson, the great English lexicographer, "What is poetry?" Johnson replied: "Why, sir, it is much easier to say what it is not."

I find it particularly auspicious that, according to Roberts and Shackleton in their book *The Canoe*, the canoe was defined by the earliest European explorers as a "vessel without decks." By what it wasn't—the un-cola of boats.   Being a 7-up drinker myself, and a person more inclined to follow instinct than reason, I take courage from this backhanded, inside-out approach to understanding.   I take Macbeth's obervation "And nothing is but what is not," for my battlecry from the bow.

Let me unbegin, then, by asking so complex a question as, "What binds the adventure to the adventurer?"   I have had this riddle variously answered by such words as "instinct," "ego," "curiosity," "courage," "mystery," and so on.   Valid responses each one of them, yet to my mind there's a link made conspicuous by its absence.   Surely, what binds the bow hunter, let's say, to the deer, is the arrow.   The arrow informs us about the nature of the hunt, the hunter and the hunted, and the intimate relationship which exists among them.   The bow hunter, unlike those in rifle gangs, operates alone.   The fact that a hunter chooses an arrow over a bullet means that he must get close to his prey.   He can only do this by learning the habits and habitat of his quarry to the point where he actually begins to look, smell and think like a deer.   He has to get inside the mind of the animal in a way which a man working in a gang outfitted with semi-automatic rifles, scopes, three-wheelers and a pack of howling black and tan hound dogs cannot.   Similarly, the canoe defines a more personal, hands-on relationship with nature reflecting a more positive, respectful wilderness attitude which the motor boat or float plane simply cannot accomplish.

What binds us irrevocably to the wilderness is the canoe, just like the arrow binds the hunter to the deer.   It makes us belong to something bigger than ourselves, not just physically, but emotionally, mentally and spiritually.   In a word, it humbles us.   The rivers of Canada are our umbilical chords linking us directly to our past, and they will be our air supply lines in the future as we embark upon the exploration of outer space.

Now, to drift for a moment in the current of this analogy, I ask all you Star Trekkies out there in Vacuum Land, where would Captain Kirk be without the USS *Enterprise?* He'd be up spaceship creek without a rocket booster is where he'd be. Lovers of high romance know a lot about Don Quixote, the Man of La Mancha, but what about his horse, Rozinante? Nay, Dorothy and Toto would still be sightseeing in Oz without the aid of her ruby shoes. "There's no place like home" is Dorothy's boon or message to Kansanians everywhere. But for us, home is not where we hang our dusty sharecropper's hat, but where we tether our trusty canoes. Adam Dollard, Canada's answer to Davey Crockett and the Alamo, found this out the hard way at the Long Sault when his canoes were the first things the Iroquois war party destroyed. Huck Finn made us laugh, but his raft set Jim free, raising the Mississippi River that "Father of Rivers" to the level of archetypal symbol and lifeblood of a lingering national myth because it is the story that makes America what it still thinks it is—the land of the free and the home of the brave. Later I shall focus on a contemporary American novel which rewrote this myth for an America ravaged from within by student unrest, civil rights protests, political assassinations, and from without by the Vietnam War.

What, therefore, is the lingering national myth of this country which constantly informs us about where we've been, where we are and where we're going? Was it the Loyalist immigrations? Was it the War of 1812-14 or the rebellions in Upper and Lower Canada in 1837? Was it the trial and execution of Louis Riel? Was it the settlement of the West symbolized by the driving of the last spike and subsequent song by Gordon Lightfoot with such romantically nationalistic lyrics as "when the green dark forest was too silent to be real?" How about Mackenzie King's seances? I see no unifying, underlying theme in these. I daresay it is the canoe.

While I was working for an Ottawa River rafting company a few years ago, my boss, the owner, suggested in the local paper that the Renfrew County Council and City of Pembroke should commission a Canadian version of Mount Rushmore, to be carved on Oiseaux Rock, a spectacular cliff face some leagues downstream from Chalk River on the Quebec side of the Ottawa.

The object was to attract tourists, of course, to the "Whitewater Capital of Canada." The faces? Who else but Sir John A. Macdonald, Samuel de Champlain and some anonymous, token Indian Chief. The boss, an American capitalist, couldn't understand why others found this idea crazy and arrogant when in his eyes the plan was perfectly reasonable and commercially sound—a potential boon to the depressed local economy. Our difference of opinion turned entirely on an environmental ethic which would not allow us to carve the face of people on the face of God.

Just as the nature of a people is largely determined by the technologies they invent and embrace, so too in literature the nature of a story is determined by the technologies, specifically the modes of transportation which are found in it. Following good scientific method, I asked a group of people—a kind of free association exercise—what type of novel they would probably be reading if imaginatively transported through the pages by:

Spaceship .... Science Fiction
U-Boat .... War Novel
Magic Carpet .... Fantasy
Covered Wagon .... Western
Hansom Cab or Taxi .... Detective

Not only were these people able to determine the type of story, they could describe the settings, characters' actions and themes associated with each novel.

What about the word canoe? Adventure, pure and simple: Canadian Precambrian arcadian adventures; Prince Andrew-and-Sarah on the Thelon River Royal adventure; mosquitoes; solitude; satisfaction; windblown lakes; rampaging rivers; illimitable forest tracts. Boundless horizons; gruelling portages—the very stuff of literature, yet sadly we observe only a few fictional titles—Mowat's *Lost In The Barrens*, Herapath's *Journey Into Danger*, Craig's *The Long Return*, Houston's *Ghost Paddle*, Grey Owl's *Sajo and Her Beaver People*. While these books are excellent reads, they remain children's stories, "Sajo" being a classic among them. Canoes, canoe trips, and voyageurs have been subject matter for historians, biologists, naturalists, biographers, autobiographers, criminologists, anthropologists, scientists, archivists, but not novelists. How odd, absurd really, that what most binds you and me to the Canadian wilderness—the canoe—that which has been central to our history, is the least understood or written about.   Haven't Englishmen written about castles and steeds?   Haven't Americans written about skyscrapers?   And cars?   Since it is only by canoe that we can properly penetrate the Canadian wilderness and since the Canadian wilderness alone defines any concept we can have of ourselves as a free and northern people, we can only conclude that our writers have missed the proverbial boat, preferring for too long the Parisian salons, New York penthouses, and London bed and breakfast lodgings to the arboreal beauty of Canada.   They believe that they can capture the spirit of Canada by getting out of it instead of into it, by saying "no" to the lonely land north of Belleville instead of "yes," as if we were ashamed of it like some huge ugly older sister; as if paddling a canoe were a degrading, primitive and uncivilized activity not to mention an inefficient waste of time.   Meanwhile, hordes of European tourists visit our wilderness areas in record numbers. Must we wait for foreigners to tell us what we've got here?   The rivers of Canada are eloquent soliloquies in the unfolding of our nation's drama.

I refuse to believe that the closest we can come to a serious fictional portrayal of the psychology of the Canadian wilderness is Margaret Atwood's *Surfacing* wherein the wilderness is coerced into working out the protagonist's personal guilt, or the French Canadian folk tale *La Chasse Galerie*, the flying canoe, where the sternsman must avoid hitting the Catholic church steeples of Quebec or the entire shantyman crew will be sent directly to purgatory.   I resent the treatment of wilderness as a come-on for ad men, as foreign investment or real estate to be bought and sold by Duddy Kravitzes who wouldn't any more step into a canoe than give a sucker an even break.

There is something special, wonderful, awe inspiring, even magical about those forests and rivers and it is the canoe that makes the magic happen.   More than one couple I know have repaired marriages or taken honeymoons out there.[4]

The magic began for me twenty years ago, the summer Sergeant Pepper taught the band to play.   I was camped on the banks of the Pickerel River off Highway 69 helping to lead a canoe trip which was part of our centennial celebrations.   I remember sitting on a rock drinking tea beside an otter slide.

The wind was sighing in the pine trees overhead as I stretched out, opening myself up to the sky. I felt good then. There was nothing theoretical or hypothetical about it. This was the most authentic, sincere and genuine gesture of my life and it is the source of the authority by which I write this essay. Little did I suspect or care or think at that time that this scene was only one among thousands of such similar experiences by Canadians past, present and future. Call it a rite of initiation, a mental landmark in what would amount to a yearly odyssey to be repeated again and again and again, so long as I had a canoe to wedge my knees into. But only recently have I tried to make sense of these experiences by bringing my education to bear down on them. I am beginning to see the canoe as having a meaning beyond what it is or what it does, not just for myself but for kindred spirits, too. The canoe has a spiritual purpose which will find its way into our literature despite our worst materialistic intentions. Grey Owl wrote:

The trail, then, is not merely a connecting link between widely distant points, it becomes an idea, a symbol of self-sacrifice, and deathless determination, an ideal to be lived up to, a creed from which none may falter.[5]

My research suggests that neither the aboriginal people, the coureurs de bois, explorers, voyageurs, traders, nor surveyors, saw value in the canoe other than what it allowed them to do largely because they did not have the written language, education, time, energy or inclination to do so. When you look at C.W. Jefferys' illustration of La Salle[6] at the Toronto carrying place in August 1681, on his way to the Mississippi, you soon get the picture. There wasn't anything romantic about travelling thousands of miles into unknown territory. That was then. This is now and our writers, because they have the time, energy, resources, education and language, have an obligation to pay tribute at least once to the real people who opened up this country by canoe and who in the process—more than their trade in whiskey, bitter crosstown rivalries, technologies, diseases, and missionary zealotry which undermined the traditional power of the medicine men—paved the way for the demise of the aboriginal inhabitants.

The canoe must be talked about not just in terms of how it handles or how it's constructed, or how it was modified to meet various needs, or where you can find a museum full of them, but what a canoe means beyond itself. A canoe isn't just an art object or self-autonomous artifact; it isn't just a "vessel without decks" any more than I'm just a body without a soul.

This observation is nothing short of revolutionary and transcendental. When an object points to an ideal, idea or creed we have the birth of a symbol and the new Canadian symbol is the canoe. When an American sees a canoe strapped to a car or float plane, he sees a canoe; a Canadian senses a way of life and he's seeing it now more than ever as our wilderness disappears.

For the novelist, the canoe as symbol is a potential gold mine of infinite possibilities. The canoeist as hero, canoe trip as structure, and wilderness as setting are naturals and uniquely Canadian. If only Mr. Canoehead could see that! If there could ever be a more perfect marriage of form, function and content in literature than the canoe trip symbolized by the canoe itself, then I have yet to read it. Our history and our wilderness have been closely connected. To the two traditional wilderness symbols of the beaver and maple leaf we must now add a third—the canoe—and it is coming at us out of the mists of our confusion about ourselves. The low-tech canoe, more than any high-tech nuclear submarine or skydome, will determine for the future generations who we are. The government may have taken our silver dollars with the canoe stamped on them out of circulation, and traded the Rocky Mountains for oil wells on our ten dollar bills, but it does not wash with the Canadian public who still feel pride in those cultural icons as things worth preserving. Our fictional heroes of the future may indeed be astronauts or nuclear submarine commanders or superstar baseball players, but the men and women of the last frontier will prevail, for civilizations define themselves (ours will be no exception) not by what they've gained or by their advances, technological or otherwise, but by what they've lost. I believe it was the 18th century French philosopher Kevlar Quarante-Neuf who said, "You don't know what you've got till it's gone." The paddle, the packsack, the Mohawk Burden strap, the wanigan, the tent, the campfire, the axe will become in the hands of our true writers the visual metaphors of an alternative way of life—tough, uncomplicated, tuned in to nature.

Canada, I maintain, will become a nation when the vanishing frontier has vanished and the canoe emerges in our literature as a symbol of a more natural way of life that has been lost and whose narrow beam points toward a national failure. The canoeist, the voyageur, as a uniquely Canadian symbol, will never die so long as we have men and women who dream of something beyond a government job. The Hudson's Bay Company may sell off its northern business interests but the 300-year-old memory of a commercial empire built on the trade of fur and on the backs of her moccasined employees shall not be diminished by time or effaced by high-rolling executives. If the North is not ours, if the Northwest Passage is not sovereign to us, then we cannot be Canadian by definition, for the dream of the Northwest Passage, like journeys through the land by canoe, makes us what we are. Mr. Canoehead, wake up and take that damn canoe off your head while you're at it. The canoe is our Conestoga wagon; the northwesterly journeys our Oregon Trail. They are our galleons riding the high seas in quest of gold. They are the most perfect statements we can make about ourselves to the rest of the world.

To help reflect on where we've been and where we are, I contrast two contemporary North American novels—one American, the other Canadian:

The river was feathering itself night and day. The rocks were full of feathers, drift on drift; even the downriver sides were steaming and bannered with them. Every shape under the river was a sick off-white; the water around us was full of little prim, dry feathers curled up like things set sail by children, all going at about the same speed we were. And out among them to the right, convoyed by six or eight feathers, was a chicken head with its glazed eye half-open, looking right at me and through me. If there had been more heads it would not have been so remarkable, but I saw only the one, going with us, turning its other eye as though the result of a movement of its gone body, drinking the sad water with a half-opened bill, pin-wheeling and floating upside down, then turning over downstream again. I half hit at it with the paddle flat, but it only moved off a foot or so and settled back into the current beside us.[7]

And later on ...

I took the knife in my fist. What? Anything. This, also, is not going to be seen. It is not ever going to be known; you can do what you want to; nothing is too terrible. I can cut off the genitals he was going to use on me. Or I can cut off his head, looking straight into his open eyes. Or I can eat him. I can do anything I have a wish to do, and I waited carefully for some wish to come; I would do what it said.

It did not come, but the ultimate horror circled me and played over the knife. I began to sing. It was a current popular favorite, a folk-rock tune. I finished, and I was withdrawn from. I straightened as well as I could. There he is, I said to him.[8]

Even the most jaded reader cannot help but be disturbed by Dickey's *Deliverance*—as brutal an examination of human nature as there ever was; an apocalyptic vision of the end of things; the death song of an America impaling itself on the thorns of barbarity and decadence, of drugs, murder, sadism and cannibalism. This is an America which has lost its way; where the hero is perceived as a head chopper in a chicken processing plant while the last of America's wild rivers, the Cahulanassee, is dammed up. The ultimate and final judgement on untamed nature. Deliverance. What else could you expect when the leader of this canoe trip, Lewis, a champion archer and outdoors enthusiast, brags to his fellow "primitives" to "bring all the liquor you like. In fact, the sensation of going down white water about half-drunk is not to be missed."

While it's true we have our drunkards and that our writers have boozed it up with the best of them, a Canadian could not have written such a novel. Canadians lack this fundamental disrespect for nature in their hearts and minds. We go beyond understandings based solely on human terms, as if we were the foci of the universe. They are simply not a part of our cultural history, heritage or traditions. Our love affair with canoes and canoeing goes back through contemporary canoeing heroes, the Grey Owls and Pauline Johnsons to a time when all North Americans lived in harmony with their surroundings. These people learned early that without the land, as James Polk says in his introduction to *Canada's Wilderness Writers*, "They are nothing."[1]

Now, let's listen to a dialogue between Rory MacDonald, a young Toronto-based immigrant and Kanina Beaverskin, a beautiful Cree native of the Hudson's Bay Lowlands. The passage is found toward the end of *The Strange One*, as Rory and Kanina prepare for a picnic encounter which will ultimately determine whether they were meant for each other:

They launched the canoe and Kanina took a paddle and climbed into the bow. Rory stepped into the stern and pushed off. The haversack of lunch was at his feet and his binoculars hung from his neck. It was good to be paddling again, to hear the gurgling slap of water caressing the canoe's resonant bottom and to feel the little craft respond like a living creature to the gentlest twist of his spruce paddle. Rory had always thought since his first experiences with canoes here in the Canadian north that the canoe was primitive man's most beautiful and most practical creation. What other conveyance can carry its heavy load as far as a waterway goes, yet be so light that it in turn can then be carried on a man's shoulders to where another waterway begins?

This was the land where, unknown centuries ago, the canoe was conceived and born. And sitting ahead of him now was one of the race who had produced it. Kanina had taken off her jacket and she was paddling now in the blue short-sleeved sweater. She paddled smoothly and gracefully, and her body swayed so that the power of her shoulders as well as her arms went into each stroke.

"You would be a very good dancer," Rory said. "I know by the way you paddle."

"My ancestors had invented the birch bark canoe before your ancestors discovered the wheel and made the first cart," she answered. "So I should know something about paddling canoes, shouldn't I?"

"I suppose you should."

"And did you ever think," she went on, "that the story of our canoe and your wheel helps explain why our races are so far apart technically today? My race had very efficient transportation by canoe while the people of your race still had to carry everything they possessed on their own backs. Yet despite our head start, history left us stranded, a primitive race still, here on the edge of the Arctic, while your race has taken possession of the world. All because the luck of history gave you the wheel."

"I don't know what you're trying to say," Rory told her. "But it sounds interesting. Why don't you start all over again?"

"Okay." Kanina laughed a little. "We had the canoe. It was perfect for the land and people who produced it, because we had lakes and rivers leading everywhere. It was a technological blind alley, so useful in its original form that there was no incentive to change or improve it. Have you got that point?"

"Yes."[9]

Although the central image and symbol of this romance is not the canoe but the Canada goose, the fact that Rory and Kanina find each other, understand each other and dare I suggest it, make love to each other, in a canoe out in the tidal flats where the Canada geese mate, is a fact of the novel not to be overlooked. What the Dickey/Bodsworth contrast demonstrates is not just a different attitude toward nature and man's technological place in it, but a way of looking at nature as expressed in the personal use of symbol and metaphor. In Lewis' hands, the breaking of his paddle is like making a death wish over a chicken bone; for Rory, the paddle signifies a noble, healthy, nature-centred way of life.

I conclude, then, by recounting the contents of a letter I received from Mr. William Hoffer, a Vancouver antiquarian who is something of a legend in his own right in the dark and mysterious book-selling world. I had written to him asking for further titles for me since he was reputed to be an expert in this field. He replied:

I must confess though I deal in Canadian literature, I am little interested in its contents. This fact is a consequence of trying again and again and always failing to find it either relevant or interesting. When the sole function of a literature is to provide material for academics it ceases to be literature. You may have to write your own Canadian version of "Deliverance" to prove your point.

A challenge for us all, to be sure, Mr. Hoffer! My response is in the works: a canoeing novel entitled *Headwaters*, but that's another story.

Notes

1 Polk, J. *Canada's Wilderness Writers*. Toronto: Clark, Irwin, and Company, 1972, p 104.

2 Campbell, J. *The Hero with a Thousand Faces*. Princeton: Princeton University Press, 1972.

3 Frye, N. *Anatomy of Criticism*. Princeton: Princeton University Press, 1968.

4 For example, Gary and Joanie McGuffin distinguished themselves as Canadians by taking a two-year paddling honeymoon in which they paddled from the Gulf of St. Lawrence to Tuktoyaktuk, 1984-85.

5 Grey Owl. *The Men of the Last Frontier*. Toronto: MacMillan, 1931.

6 Jefferys, C.W. *The Picture Gallery of Canadian History*. Toronto: Ryerson Press, 1942.

7 Dickey, J. *Deliverance*. Boston: Houghton Mifflin Company, 1970, p 86.

8 Dickey, p 206.

9 Bodsworth, F. *The Strange One*. New York: Dodd, Mead, and Company, 1959, pp 215-6.

Lilly Dipping it Ain't

Kenneth G. Roberts

People of young nations tend to be restless and roving. The men may have their hand on the plough, but their eyes are more likely to be on the distant hills and their minds may be speculating on what lies beyond the horizon. So it was in Canada.

But rovers, adventurers, and explorers had to have conveyance in a land without roads. In the United States it was the horse and the covered wagon that stamped their image on the psyche of the American people. In Canada, it was the canoe. Until the railway was punched through to the West, the canoe remained the fastest means of crossing Canada.

We seem to have forgotten so much of our heritage, so much of the detail of how people travelled to open up this enormous land, so much of the technique of canoe travel. Yet the paddle, the pole, the line and the sail were topics of daily concern and ingenuity in the minds of our forebears. Perhaps we should look at them in more detail, for these were among the realities of daily life. As such, they form part of the Canadian cultural heritage.

There were, and are, six fairly distinct ways of propelling a canoe: paddling it; poling it through tranquil waters or against swift current or controlling its downstream speed with setting poles; tracking it upstream or lining it downstream from the shore at the end of a length of rope or rawhide babiche; sailing it with a fair wind; getting into the water and dragging or manhandling it up against the current; and, when all these failed, portaging it or carrying it around a rapid or obstruction, or between different drainage systems. But situations arose where all these failed; where the water was too swift for the paddle, too deep for the pole or for a man to wade and drag the

canoe, where there was no passage along the shore for a man
to walk and track the canoe, and where the banks of the river
were too precipitous for a portage. Frequently, under such desperate conditions, the canoe was dragged upstream by pulling
on the branches of overhanging trees.

With the exception of dragging, all of these methods of
canoe travel demanded specialized equipment and well developed techniques, and among these the paddle takes precedence
over them all.

The design of a paddle incorporates many, many factors,
and the combinations of these factors result in an unbelievable
variety of shapes and refinements.

Paddle design depends to a large extent on the position
of the paddler in a canoe: whether the paddler is standing up
as many Indians did in Central America; or sitting on a canoe
stool as some did on the Northwest Coast; or kneeling on the
bottom or sitting on their heels as did many Woodland Indians;
or sitting on the bottom with legs outstretched as was customary
among Woodland Indian women.

The design of the single paddle depends on how the
paddler actually works his paddle; a person who uses the J-
stroke or the Canadian stroke or a pitch stroke to control the
veer of a canoe must have a grip or a crutch handle at the top
of the shaft to control the pitch of the blade. The design of a
paddle is also influenced by whether the paddler levers the paddle off the gunwale or constantly holds it free of the canoe during
the stroke. The design is influenced as well by the size and
strength of the paddler, by the average freeboard of the canoe
and, in some cultures, by whether the paddle was to be used by
a man or a woman. It depends on the function of the paddler:
whether to simply provide motive power, whether a bowman
with a wide reaching paddle in a freight canoe, or a sternman
with a long steering paddle; or whether to rudder when under
sail; or whether hunting or at war and a completely dripless silence is required; or whether racing, and short bursts of furious
power are needed, or cruising and putting in a 12- to 16-hour
day on the water. Design depends upon the woods available:
the shaft and blade of a cedar paddle must be left thick to give
them strength; the dense wood of the ash or hickory must be
fined thin to reduce the paddle's weight; the curly grain of
birdseye maple makes a paddle blade that is almost unsplitable

so that it can be fined thin to give it a whip at the end of a stroke; the yew of the West Coast was tough and springy and could be knifed thin and light; spruce was a popular inland wood because it was light and easy to work but unsatisfactory in that the blade split easily; and cherry was a beautiul wood in its own right, straight-grained and warm in colour, light in weight and with a whip to it when thinned down. Blades made of any of these woods might demand a spine down the centre to increase their strength or, in the case of the weaker woods, a single-faced blade with back left thick for strength.

Since a paddle was frequently a personal tool, the need for identification became a problem, particularly in a social group in which the basic design was the same. If one can visualize a small beach on the Northwest Coast with fifty or sixty Makah canoes pulled up on the sand, it is not unreasonable to suppose that there might have been more than a thousand paddles in the village. Or if one can recreate in the mind's eye the bustling scene at Grand Portage at the head of Lake Superior when the loads of merchandise from perhaps fifty *canots du maître* were being broken down for the smaller *canots du nord*, with more than one thousand paddles scattered among the bark canoes, it becomes obvious that some form of paddle identification was a necessity.

Sometimes there was group identification. Often, the paddles in a specific freight canoe of the fur trade were painted with the same design or colour to show that they belonged to that particular outfit. Then, the individual voyageurs would add their own personal marks to their own paddles. On the Northwest Coast, as among the Haida, Kwakiutl and Nootka, the paddles were often elaborately scribed and painted with figurative images of animals and birds and fish, some to placate the spirits of the animal world, some to proclaim clan affiliations, and some to satisfy shamanistic beliefs. To a visitor they might have all appeared the same but, to the practiced eye, they were each different and identifiable. One beautifully decorated Kwakiutl paddle from the 19th century is signed "Yakuglas" on the flat loom below the crutch handle. He had reason to be proud of his paddle.

The Malacite, Micmac and Passamaquoddy Indians of the East Coast all preferred leaf and vine designs, often scribed into the wood with a sharp tool or burned into the surface with a hot iron. The Malacite owner frequently incised his personal mark, or *dupskodegun*, on the flat of his paddle near the grip. On the Northwest Coast, many tribes used the iridescent shell of abalone for inlaying their ceremonial paddles.

Of all the forms of decoration and identification, designs in paints and dyes were most widely used. While very few of the pre-contact paddles have survived, we do know from first accounts by Europeans and from archaeology that colour was highly appreciated among the North American Indians, and that dyes and pigment were an important item of their trade. The first recorded Europeans to see the Beothuks of Newfoundland labelled them "red Indians" because of their use of red ochre to cover themselves, their weapons and their tools—including their paddles. In various parts of the Continent, other ochres and pigments gave the Indians tints of brown, red, green, blue, yellow, orange and purple. Black, for example, was achieved by scorching and oiling wood, by grinding charcoal or soot into fats and animal glues, by mixing ground graphite with clear gums, by using black bitumen or, among the Eskimos, combining charcoal and blood.

Canoe paddles were constantly breaking. Alexander Mackenzie, returning from his exploration of the river that bears his name, was constantly replacing broken paddles. "After having passed the carrying places," he wrote, "we encamped at the Dog River, at half past four in the afternoon, in a state of great fatigue. The canoe was again gummed, and paddles were made to replace those that had been broken in ascending the rapids." On yet another day, "One of my Indians having broken his paddle, attempted to take one of theirs (Dogribs) which was immediately contested by its owner, and on my interfering to prevent this act of injustice, he manifested his gratitude to me on the occasion. We lost an hour and a half in this conference." Later on, Mackenzie writes, "The people made themselves paddles and repaired the canoe. It is an extraordinary circumstance for which I do not pretend to account, that there is some peculiar quality in the water of this river, which corrodes wood, from the destructive effect it had on the paddles."[1]

But all paddles were not made in the bush, or by the voyageurs themselves in the winter months. By the late 18th century, mass production of paddles for the fur trade was an estabished industry in Quebec. In a contract of 1780, Joseph

Hubert *dit* Lacroix, a fur trade merchant of Montreal, contracted to have a habitant, Amable Delorme, make 2,000 paddles. In another deal in 1781, the merchant Richard Dobie let a contract to Joseph Perrault of Champlain, Quebec, to make 1,000 paddles. And there are hundreds more big contracts like this scattered through the old records of the Quebec notaries. Under these circumstances, with the mass-produced paddles fanning out through hundreds of cultures in North America, it would seem likely that many local designs would disappear. Some certainly did, but many Indians and whites clung tenaciously to the style of paddle that best suited them and their individual tastes and requirements. Even today one can stimulate a lively campfire argument among canoe enthusiasts simply by extolling one paddle design at the expense of another.

The double-bladed paddle was predominantly an Eskimo tool and it likely evolved because of the very low seating arrangement in a kayak. It is very awkward to paddle a one-holed kayak with a single-bladed paddle; however, while the low seating position in a kayak almost dictates a double paddle, a double paddle does not necessarily mean that the paddler has to sit with outstretched legs.

In the basin of the Yukon River, early travellers have reported small Indian kayaks being paddled with a double paddle, and even the occasional bark canoe, but these instances can be directly attributed to the close intermingling of the Indian and Eskimo cultures in the area.

Because the Eskimo had to rely largely on driftwood as a material for his double paddle, and consequently had to design each individual product to the quality of his material, there was considerable variation in design, even within one community.

While paddles were ideally suited to propelling a canoe most of the time, there were many waterways that were either too shallow for efficient paddling or in which the current was too swift to be stemmed with the paddle. In areas where very shallow water was normal, or where ponderous craft were being moved, a pole (or *perche* among the French Canadians) was often the preferred tool.

Even in the woodlands, the traditional paddle was sometimes discarded for the pole in still, shallow water. A Chipewyan man would pole his wife in a bark canoe into the shallow rice swamps, positioning her so that she could reap the wild grain by knocking it from the standing rice stalks into the canoe.

It didn't take the newly arrived Europeans long to see the advantages of the pole and to adopt it—like the canoe and the paddle—for their own use. As early as 1613, Samuel de Champlain was exploring up the Ottawa River with four Frenchmen and an Indian. After passing the Chats Falls he wrote, "Continuing our journey we passed two other rapids, one by portaging, and the other by paddling and pushing on the bottom with poles."[2]

On his way up the Peace River, Simon Fraser wrote at one point, "The water was rather low when we left the Portage (Rocky Mountain Portage) but it is now rising faster. However, though we seldom make use of the paddles, the bottom being good it is good going by the pole." A few days later he complains, "In the afternoon we passed a strong rapid at a point which gave us much trouble to ascend, on account of the Rocks being perpendicular, and no bottom for the poles."[3]

In the journal of his exploration of the Mackenzie River, Alexander Mackenzie mentions poles frequently. At one point he says, "It rained throughout the night and till twelve this day; while the business of preparing great and small poles, and putting the canoe in order, caused us to remain till five in the afternoon."[4] This suggests that two sizes of poles were cut, one probably for fast, shallow water and one for deep water.

Most writers who have described poling have neglected to describe the poles in any detail. There were several factors that had to be considered in selecting suitable material. They had to be reasonably light for long hours of work; straight so they wouldn't bend under strain; strong so that they would not break in the middle of a rapid; and smooth so that they would slide through the hands easily. The pushing end was often burned to prevent fraying and splitting and, later, the Europeans shod them with iron for the same reason. In the north, spruce was the preferred wood because of its even taper, and about ten feet seemed to be the ideal length.

The artist Arthur Heming, travelling with a band of Chipewyans early in this century, described a fairly typical use of poles when he arrived at the foot of a rapid:

This Oo-koo-hoo and Amik examined carefully from the river bank, and decided it could be ascended by poling. So from green wood we cut suitable poles of about two inches in diameter and from seven to nine feet in length and knifed them carefully to rid them of bark and knots. Then, for this was a shoal rapids, both bow person and stern person stood up, the better to put the full force of their strength and weight into the work; the children, however, merely knelt to the work of wielding their slender poles; but in deep water, or where there were many boulders and consequently greater risk if the canoe were overturned, all would have knelt to do the work.

Going bow-on straight for the mid-stream current, we plied our poles to good advantage. Each man remembered, however, to lift his pole only when his mate's had been planted firmly in the river bottom. Then he would fix his own a little farther ahead and throw all his weight and strength upon it, while at the same moment his companion went the same round. Then he would firmly re-fix his pole a little farther up stream, and then once again shoved in unison. It was hard but joyous work, for standing up in a canoe surrounded by a powerful and treacherous current gave us the thrill of adventure.[5]

Canoes were eased down rapids by setting poles too, a more cautious descent than running them. In the big bark freight canoes of the fur trade, six or eight poles could be set against the bottom to slow the canoe down in fast water and ease it through tight channels of a rapid which would have otherwise been dangerous.

When the water was too swift or too deep to stem by the pole, Indians and Europeans in the northern half of the Continent resorted to pulling the canoe through the rapids at the end of a line. This was variously called lining, tracking or cordelling. It may sound simple but it demands a great deal of knowledge about water and considerable technique to do well and safely, as Samuel de Champlain found out during his first trip up the Ottawa:

...being unable to portage our canoes on account of the thickness of the woods, we had to track them, and in pulling mine I nearly lost my life, because the canoe turned broadside into a whirlpool, and had I not luckily fallen between two rocks, the canoe would have dragged me in, since I could not quickly enough loosen the rope which was twisted round my hand, which hurt me very much, and nearly cut it off. In this danger I cried aloud to God and began to pull my canoe toward me, which was sent back to me by an eddy such as occurs in these rapids.[6]

The biggest problem in tracking a canoe is to keep it in deep water. To do this, one or two people were often left in the canoe to steer it with a paddle or to fend off the shore with a pole. Sometimes a freight canoe was taken up *demi-charge*, or half-loaded, and sometimes empty to reduce the strain on the lines and on the men hauling on them on shore.

Generally, the lines of braided rawhide were about a hundred feet long, but Alexander Mackenzie mentions lines three and four times that length during his northern exploration. At one point, his men were tracking the canoe up some very fast water when they ran out of tow path, with the river running along a perpendicular rock wall. He wrote:

...I desired, however, two of the men to take the line, which was seventy fathoms in length, with a small roll of bark, and endeavour to climb up the rocks, from whence they were to descend on the other side of that which opposed our progress; they were then to fasten the end of the line to the roll of bark, which the current would bring to us; this being effected, they would be able to draw us up. This was an enterprise of difficulty and danger, but it was crowned with success; though to get to the water's edge above, the men were obliged to let themselves down with the line, run round a tree, from the summit of the rock. By a repetition of the same operation, we at length cleared the rapid, with the additional trouble of carrying the canoe, and unloading at two cascades.[7]

Frederick Schwatka observed that the Indians tracked their canoes against the current in two ways, each requiring two men. In the first,

...an Indian pulls the canoe with a rope while a companion just in his rear and following in his footsteps keeps the head of the canoe in the stream, with a long pole at just such distance as he may desire according to the obstacles that are presented. If the water from the bank for some distance out, say twelve or fifteen feet, is clear of all obstacles, his companion will fall in the rear as his pole will allow and assist the rope person by pushing upstream, but in shallow, swift places he has all he can do to regulate the canoe's course through the projecting stones, and the burden of the draft falls on the rope person.[8]

The other method involves two men equipped with long poles. The end of the lead man's pole is fixed to the bow of the canoe, and the end of his companion's pole to the stern. Walking along the bank, with the canoe slightly upstream, the two men provided the motive power by pushing, and a fair degree of control to guide it through rocks and obstructions.

The prehistoric use of sail by native people has been a matter for considerable debate. It seems incomprehensible that the North American Indian did not take advantage of a following wind with some form of sail before the arrival of the Europeans. Yet, when all the written evidence is examined closely in relation to dates, the probability or possibility of previous contacts with Europeans, the reliability of the observers, and the alignment with the facts of archaeology, it would appear that true sails were not known in pre-Columbian North America except perhaps among the Eskimo of the Western Arctic and the Maya of Yukatan.

The first person to leave a good record of the Eskimos in Davis Strait in the Arctic Waters between Greenland and Baffin Island was Martin Frobisher in 1576. Chronicling the voyage and the lifestyle of the Eskimos they met, Christopher Hall wrote,

Those beasts, fishes, and foules, which they kill, are their meat, drinke, apparell, houses, bedding, hose, shooes, threed, and sailes for their boates ... They have one sort of greater boates wherein they can carrie aboue twentie persons, and haue a Mast with a saile thereon, which saile is made of thinne skinnes or bladders sowed together with the sinews of fishes.

Certainly, at that date, the Eskimos were using sail, and certainly their inventiveness was so extraordinary that they might very well have devised their sails for themselves. When the Vikings first arrived in Greenland in the 9th century they found Christian refugees from Ireland already settled there, and the Viking settlements in Greenland had lasted for more than 400 years after that. Only archaeology can tell us whether the Eastern Eskimos had sails of their own before the arrival of Europeans.

In the advanced canoe culture of the Northwest Coast, the native peoples appear to have adopted the sail from their European visitors. When Captain Cook arrived in Nootka Sound in 1778, he described the canoes in some detail and then wrote that the Indians "...have acquired great dexterity in managing those paddles by constant use, for sails are no part of their navigation."9 This is supported by John Meares who arrived in Nootka Sound ten years later. "After we had been in King George's (Nootka) Sound," he reported, "the natives began to make use of sails made of mats, in imitation of ours. We had, indeed, rigged up one of Hanna's (a chief from Clarjoquot Sound) canoes for him with a pendant etc., etc., of which he was proud beyond measure..."10

Four years later, 1792, Joseph Ingraham, captain of the Boston brigantine *Hope*, was sailing along the west coast of Vancouver Island, and wrote in his journal, "... we passed a vaste number of canoes, every one with a sail, which was a new thing for me, as I never saw them make use of any in this part before." And Ingraham was no newcomer to the coast; he had spent ten months in Nootka Sound in 1788 and 1779.

On the other hand, the ethnologist Franz Boas, working among the Kwakiutl Indians, wrote: "It seems that the Northwest Coast Indians had sails before the advent of the whites."11 And in his reports, he spends considerable time describing a sail made of thin wooden planks laced together, which was propped up against the mast. Considering the fact that many of the coastal tribes used their canoes in tandem to carry their house planks between their permanent villages and their summer camps, and the fact that they sometimes raised a house plank to catch a following wind on this very stable craft, the lighter and broader wooden sail would appear to have developed from this practice.

Among the Woodland Indians essentially the same situation seems to have existed. In their bark canoes and dugouts the Indians may have taken advantage of a following wind by holding up a small evergreen tree in the bow of the canoe, but there are no reliable reports of this until long after the Europeans had been in contact with them.

The adoption of the concept of sail was not always the idea of the Indians; French Jesuit missionaries were urging them to use sail. Father Le Jeune explained in 1634 that,

... he would sail with them (the Indians) must know how to handle the paddle; and, as it is hard work, especially at first, when one is not accustomed to it, we give to every Canoe in which any of our Fathers embark a large sheet which serves as sail, to relieve them from this work; but, although these Barbarians may be told that this sail is the Father's paddle, that they do not wield any others, they do not fail sometimes to make them take one of wood, which has to be well worked, to satisfy them.[12]

With the promotion of sail as active as this, the dissemination of the idea could have been as rapid as the travels of missionaries and explorers themselves.

As the years went on, most Indian canoe people recognized sailing as a useful relaxation from paddling, and by the 19th century canoe sailing was so widespread a practice that both Indians and Europeans accepted it as a normal routine. Nervous newcomers to canoe travel, however, to whom canoe sailing was a dubious mode of transport, were intrigued by the sails and left us some colourful descriptions.

One observer wrote in 1850 that a big Micmac seagoing canoe, nearly 24 feet long, carried seventeen yards of sail, and the owners bragged about the speed they could attain.

The artist George Catlin said that, among the Sioux, a man would sometimes stand in a canoe facing the paddler and hold a blanket spread out as a sail. One sketch he made of the scene shows a whole fleet of canoes with spread blankets, as though they are racing for the sheer fun of it.

As early as 1684, the Baron de Lahontan was writing of the "Canadians" and their use of sail. Speaking of big, bark canoes of about 28 feet, he wrote:

When the season serves, they carry little Sails; but if the Wind be but a little brisk, tho' they run afore it, 'tis impossible to make any use of it without running the risque of Ship-wrack. If their course lies directly South, they cannot put up Sail without the wind stands at one of the eight points, between North-West and North-East; and if a wind happens to spring any where else, (unless it comes from the Land which they coast along) they are oblig'd to put in to the shoar with all possible expedition, and unload the Boat out of hand, till such time as a calm returns.[13]

With the evidence at hand, all we can really say is that the Western Eskimos used sails before the arrival of Europeans; that the Woodland Indians almost certainly adopted the European idea and used it for more than three hundred years; and that the Indians on the Northwest Coast used it from about eighteen hundred until they abandoned the canoe for European craft in the 20th century. Yet, despite all the negative reports, we still suspect that the Indians of North America probably used crude sails before the arrival of Europeans. After all, many of them were superb boatmen and spent a large part of their lives on the water. In their migrations many of them carried in their canoes large roles of bark and matting for their lodges, large planks of wood for their houses, buffalo skins for their teepees and, in the south, well woven sheets of cotton. Somewhere, somehow, individuals must have taken advantage of a following wind.

When paddle and pole and line failed as a mode of propulsion for the canoe travellers, they resorted to dragging. This simply meant going overboard and wading, pulling the canoe against the current, hand guiding it between rocks, half lifting it over shallow riffles, lining it upstream from the bed of the river, and fending it clear of ice on the river bank. In the icy waters of spring or during the frosty days of autumn travel, it was chilling work and dangerous for the feet and ankles on a rock-strewn bottom. When there was a lot of shallow water to be navigated, as in the Maritime Provinces, the Indians would sometimes lash long strips of wood to the bottom of the canoe to protect the bark. But for human beings there was no protection. After a day of walking in "water as cold as ice", the legs and feet of Mackenzie's men were so benumbed one evening that he was "apprehensive about the consequences." Rheumatism was a common affliction among both Indians and seasoned voyageurs.

Writing to Quebec in 1635, the Jesuit Father Brébeuf described how the Indians negotiated swift water:

Some places, where the current is not less strong than in these rapids, although easier at first, the Savages get into the water, and haul and guide by hand their canoes with extreme difficulty and danger: for they sometimes get in up to the neck, and are compelled to let go their hold, saving themselves as best they can from the rapidity of the water, which snatches from them and bears off their canoe. I kept count of the number of portages, and found that we carried our canoes thirty five times, and dragged them at least fifty. I sometimes took a hand in helping the Savages, but the bottom of the river is full of stones, so sharp that I could not walk long, being barefooted.[14]

The big advantage of a bark or skin canoe was that they were light enough to be carried considerable distances. This allowed travellers to portage their craft around an obstruction in the river and to continue their voyage on the other side. This was an enormous advantage over dugouts and the heavy boats of Europeans which were rarely carried any distance. But there were drawbacks to the portage too; sometimes the terrain alongside a rapid would be so rugged, or swampy, or precipitous that the portage would become a nightmare. This was particularly so during the operations of the fur trade when every 90-pound *pièce* of trade goods and every bale of fur had to be carried over the portages too. On some portages a voyageur might have to make the overland trip five times — three of them loaded.

Virtually everyone who has travelled by bark canoe has a horror story to tell about some portage, and Captain John Palliser was no exception. En route between York Factory on Hudson Bay and the country he was to survey west of Lake Superior in 1857, he and his party of voyageurs reached the Savannah Portage on the Nelson River: "The greater portion of this desperate portage is over dreary swamp," he wrote:

Through which the men, loaded as they are, (each with nearly 200 lbs. on his back,) have the greatest difficulty struggling. It is, perhaps, not quite so long as the Prairie Portage, but far more formidable; it would be impassable but for trees and logs of wood along which the men walk and so avoid sinking to their middle in the swamp; but in many places these planks were rotten, and the poor fellows had to use desperate exertions to extricate themselves. No accidents, however, occurred here to either men, or instruments, while carrying the baggage over this arduous portage, for the greatest labour, however, is the carrying the canoes, which is the severest test of strength and endurance.[15]

The small bark hunting canoes of the Indians were often carried like a basket, with the arm of the owner crooked under a thwart. Larger, family canoes were sometimes carried right side up with the bow and stern of the canoe sitting on the shoulders of the carriers. The *canots du nord* were also carried in this way. The larger *canots du maître* were generally carried upside down with two men toward the bow and two toward the stern with the gunwales resting on their shoulders.

Most of the contents of the canoes were carried with a tump line, a broad band of leather looped over the forehead of the carrier and thinning down to a strap looped under the load which rested on his back and shoulders. Enormous burdens could be carried in this way, and the fur trade voyageurs often crossed the portages at a jog-trot. Lt. William F. Butler, special agent for Colonel Garnet Wolsey during the Canadian Red River Expedition, was fascinated by all aspects of canoe travel, including portages. He wrote:

The Grand Portage which is three quarters of a mile in length, is the great test of strength of the Indian and half-breed; but, if (Alexander) Mackenzie speaks correctly, the voyageur has much degenerated since the eary days of the fur trade, for he writes that seven pieces, weighing each ninety pounds, were carried over the Grand Portage by an Indian in one trip—630 pounds borne three quarters of a mile by one man—the loads look big enough still, but 250 pounds is considered excessive now (1870). These loads are carried in a manner which allows the whole strength of the body to be put into the work. A broad leather strap is placed around the forehead, the ends of the strap passing back over the shoulders support the pieces which, thus carried, lie along the spine from the small of the back to the crown of the head. When fully loaded, the voyageur stands with his body bent forward, and with one hand steadying the "pieces", he trots briskly away over the steep and rock-strewn portage, his bare or moccasined feet enable him to pass nimbly over the slippery rocks in places where boots would infallibly send the portager and pieces feet-foremost to the bottom.[16]

From the subtle and efficient to the downright brutish, Canadian canoe travellers through the centuries have seized whatever method would move the craft effectively and with least effort. Still today, pole and sail survive with paddle, line and portage as the means to link the vessel and the person to the waterway. The renewed interest in paddle design and ornamentation shows that this aspect of canoeing continues to be a part of Canadian culture.

Notes

1   Mackenzie, A. *Voyages from Montreal, on the River St. Lawrence through the Continent of of North America, to the Frozen and Pacific Oceans; in the Years 1789 and 1793.* Philadelphia: Morgan, 1802.

2   Champlain, S. *Voyages of Samuel de Champlain, Vol. III, 1611-1618.* Boston: Prince Society, 1882.

3 Fraser, S. *The Letters and Journals of Simon Fraser.* Toronto: Macmillan, 1960.

4 Mackenzie, op. cit.

5 Tyrrell, J.W. (with Arthur Henry Howard Heming). *Across the Sub-Arctics of Canada, a Journey of 3,200 Miles by Canoe and Snowshoe through the Barren Lands.* Toronto: Briggs, 1897.

6 Champlain, op. cit.

7 Mackenzie, op. cit.

8 Schwatka, F. *In the Hyperborean Regions: a Trip within the Arctic Circle.* Microfiche filmed from a copy of the original publication held by the Library Division, Provincial Archives of British Columbia. Ottawa: Canadian Institute for Historical Microreproductions, 1982.

9 Cook, J. *A Journal of a Voyage Round the World in H.M. Ship Endeavour, in the Years 1768, 1770, and 1771.* Amsterdam: N. Israel, 1967.

10 Meares, J. *Voyages Made in the Years 1788 and 1789 from China to the N.W. Coast of America.* London: Logographic Press, 1791.

11 Boas, Franz. *Kwakiutl Ethnography.* Chicago: University of Chicago Press, 1966.

12 LeJeune, P. *Relation du Voyage fait a Canada pour la prise de possession du fort de Quebec par les François.* Ottawa: Library of the Public Archives of Canada, microfiche, undated.

13 Catlin, G. *Life among the Indians.* London: Gall and Inglis, 1841.

14 Brébeuf, J. *The Travels and Sufferings of Father Jean de Brébeuf among the Hurons of Canada as Described by Himself.* London: The Golden Cockerel Press, 1938.

15 Palliser, J. *Solitary Rambles and Adventures of a Hunter in the Prairies.* Edmonton: Hurtig, 1969.

16 Butler, W.F. *Great Lone Land: A Narrative of Travel and Adventure in the North-west of America,* (5th ed.). London: Low, 1873.

Canoe Trips:
Doors to the Primitive

Bert Horwood

A wrong sound penetrated my sleep. I roused and listened to the unending rattle of the rain on the tent, the dripping water from the laden pine boughs beyond. It was the blackest of nights, calm, but wringing with rain. Then faintly, the metallic shrill of the whistle came again. Damn! I struggled up, pulled on damp clothing, wet socks and boots (loathsome things), and rain gear, and crawled out into the black wetness. A high school student on solo had signalled for help, and it was my task to provide it as well as prevent unnecessary general alarms and whistles throughout the entire forest. Feeling my way gently down the esker ridge, I found the canoe and slipped it into the water. Rain sounds now changed to the sibilance of determined fine drops on a still lake, and I pushed off. The whistle trilled again, giving me the fix I needed to paddle easily across the bay to the solo site I had carefully selected for Nancy. "Nancy," I called quietly, "it's Bert. I'm coming to your camp." "Oh. Okay," said a small voice. An hour later, after much talk of beaver raids on her camp, attempts at suicide, throwing up in bed and other topics well suited to the darkest hours of the wettest night, Nancy settled down in her snug tarp shelter to try to sleep, and I returned to base to do the same.

This incident illustrates both the hazards and the promise of wilderness experience. The fundamental encounter of the alienated person with the primitive experience long denied opens doors for the discovery of the kinds of relationships with which humans evolved and without which rich, full lives cannot be led.

Canoe trips provide openings through which 20th century youths may recover profoundly important aspects of their instinctual, Stone Age inheritance. The process of alienation is real, but it is at least partially reversible—wilderness experiences can contribute to culture by promoting the growth of relationships otherwise lost in alienation.

White water trips in particular have potential to open doors for youths to the primitive world from which their breeding has alienated them. At the most superficial levels, the canoe trip provokes a new awareness of the body and its relationship to the natural world. The fundamental physiological needs to eat, sleep, eliminate, and keep warm take on new meanings. More profoundly, young participants come to encounter fear, pain, joy and elation in new ways. Social relationships are also enhanced.

Four aspects of canoe tripping, as done by the Trekkers, (the outing club of Mackenzie High School in Deep River, Ontario) have particularly high potential for encounters with the primitive: the weather; the night; the river; and relationships with others. The weather, because the usual life of civilized persons is one of escape and evasion from the elements; the night, because our culture is a dark-shunning, light-clinging one; the river, because it is the most effective stimulus of healthy fear and pain; interpersonal relationships, because canoe trippers find themselves isolated from the civilized pattern of limited interaction. Other aspects could also be effective if canoe trips were to be taken with more primitive technology. For example, to travel with a minimum of food and to live off the land would bring hunger as a primitive experience unknown to Canadian youth. Most canoe groups, including Mackenzie Trekkers, travel with excellent equipment and generous victualling, so this particular form of primitive encounter is not present.

Children are taught from their earliest time to dress properly and to "come in out of the rain." One of the inevitable challenges for civilized youth outdoors is to be able to function in weather which would send them scurrying for shelter at home. Students report a strong feeling of disbelief when the exigencies of travel first require them to make a fire, cook and eat, break camp and travel under the steady drizzle which has already soaked most of their gear. This must be what part of our lost Stone Age was like. And to recover even a rudimentary level of ability to cope opens a door to the lost realm. A major part of our heritage, found in this way, is not only the competence to endure, but also the ability to get warm and dry when you are wet and cold.

Meeting the weather on a sustained basis is an important opportunity to rediscover the primitive on canoe trips. It is common to observe novices scrambling feverishly for their rain clothing when the first tentative drops begin to fall from even a sunny sky. When the threatened rain fails to develop, they re-pack the protective clothing, only to repeat the process a short while later. Part of our alienation lies in unrealistic fear of the weather. And part of the difficulty in dealing with it is that there is wisdom in that fear. To the extent that young persons learn to distinguish the two, and become able to know when to hide and when to proceed and how, closer relationship and identity with the natural world is established.

Darkness and night are potentially powerful aspects of canoe trips through which people can encounter the primitive. The primal dependence on fire, even transcending utility for cooking and warmth, provides an opportunity to explore primitive relationships normally not accessible at home. To sleep on the earth with only a thin pad and sleeping robe, to have the slender partition of nylon as the sole barrier to the night noises and the nameless scurrying; these are the doors to the primitive world which can not be opened any other way.

Roderick Nash[1] describes the connection between images of darkness and European images of wilderness. He argues that the rejection of wilderness by civilized people is based on the restricted visibility in the primeval forest. Being able to see clearly and far was a central requirement associated with prediction and control of the environment. The wilderness forests of North America restrict vision and they are described as dark and dangerous. In the same way, the dark of night is given qualities of danger for the alienated youth. To explore the outer darkness has potential for the exploration of the inner darkness for which it is a metaphor.

The river itself is a teacher because of its neutrality and implacability. It is the most inescapable primitive element on a canoe trip. In the thrust and curl of white water or in the aching, dangerous monotony of big lake waves, alienated young people find that they are driven inexorably to find new relationships and new levels of understanding about themselves and their relationships to each other and the world. The driving emotions are fear and euphoria, the two being mutually dependent. The enfolding sensation is pain. It is very difficult, especially for novices, to conceal fear at the top of rapids. No one tries to hide the euphoria at the end of the run. Here again, a door is opened for the discovery of lost relationships. After a very difficult dump a student said, "I was really angry with myself for coming. I wanted either to die or go home." This melodramatic statement showed the strength of feeling aroused in an otherwise passive individual.

Pain is an almost continuous companion in the early stages of a hard trip. There is a tendency for students to deny it. But the appearance of occasional blisters, the complaints, ill-temper and hard breathing on portages and, finally, the conversation of staff members about aching muscles bring the existence of pain into public scrutiny. Several kinds of lessons are learned: the first surprising one is that some kinds of pain can't be easily escaped, as with a kiss or a pill; another is that it is possible to continue to function effectively, even enjoy moments, while hurting. Students were astonished to learn that staff members ached and hurt, and were willing to talk about it. Validation of the pain experience due to necessary, unaccustomed, hard physical labour enables students, given the opportunity, to talk about their methods for dealing with it. A new, previously unknown dimension of relationship to themselves and the world has been discovered.

The most important changes students experience in interpersonal relationships are shifts from a self-centred point of view to a perspective which takes others into account.[2] The nature and meaning of friendship changes as the dynamics of friendship change from city ones, where disagreements are solved by escape, to more authentic ones imposed by inescapable proximity and the need to be functional. Students reveal substantial insight into their own development of new kinds of interactions and speech patterns. The absence of parents from this phase of growth is extremely important. The students must rely on their own resources to solve interpersonal problems. There is no place to hide from difficult encounters when protective parents are out of reach.

Occasionally, the absence of the restraints of civilization, including parents, results in wildly erratic behaviour. It can be difficult to understand why students sometimes noisily, energetically and creatively break the norms of accepted behaviour on the trail or in camp. It is tempting to treat such lapses as simple breaches of discipline ("being bad") and respond appropriately. But there is another way of looking at it. Students may well be exhibiting very crude sensitivity to the trickster archetype.[3] They may be naturally celebrating and exploring their liberty to be other than they are. The invariable lack of malice and universal presence of humour in such incidents support the possibility that trickster may be lurking nearby.

This possibility points out the gap existing between the potential of canoe trips and the actual rediscovery of relationship. In my experience, deviant behaviour is treated appropriately as a breach of discipline and never as an opportunity to explore the meaning of trickster in the world. Canoe trip leaders could do much to guide students into the hidden realms, to penetrate more deeply through the barriers of alienation into richer and more fully realized relationships.

The extent to which teachers and instructors should attempt this very serious work has been a subject of intense debate.[4] For some, the canoe trip experience speaks for itself. No interpretation is required for participants to gain whatever benefits there may be. For others, the experience is a powerful starting point for further development. Mackenzie Trekkers organizers mostly practice the former position. But the potential for adopting a deliberately active stance is there, too. The power of the experiences to push the young toward rediscovered relationships lies in the metaphoric connections of the physical events to other aspects of life.

Many writers and educators have considered the gap between face value and the potential metaphoric power experience, all heeding the admonition of Dag Hammarskjold who said, "Never for the sake of peace and quiet deny your experience or convictions."

In the powerful novel, *Dreamspeaker*,[5] a terrified child is treated for his violent psychotic behaviour. While well-intentioned, hospital treatment denies the child's spiritual experience. He runs away and is found cold and hungry by a Nootka Indian elder and his companion, who feed, shelter, and come to know the boy like none of his traditional therapists. The boy recounts stories of mental torment and agonizing visions. To his surprise, the older man not only accepts the dreams, but has names for the frightening creatures in them. He teaches the boy how to cope with the spirits, what songs to sing, what dances to dance.

In this book, there is a striking contrast between the civilized and primitive treatments of the boy. In the one, denial of his experience makes him more confused and desperate. In the other, validation of the experience empowers the boy in both spiritual and material worlds. Unfortunately, as one might expect—and as portent of the danger in denying the spiritual in our cultural practices—the story ends with the boy's enforced return to an institution and his terrorized self-destruction.

No less vividly, R.D. Laing in *The Politics of Experience* describes the tensions and distortions needed to bring each Stone Age baby born today out of its state of wild and primitive humanity into the madness we know as modern civilization. He contends that there are virtues of primitiveness which have been lost as the price of the hard-learned vices of civilization. The result is alienation. Laing goes on to say that modern humans are fundamentally alienated from themselves, their fellows and their world. But, as Laing shows, we are not born that way. Rather, we are born with a highly evolved potential for attachment and engagement with the worlds of matter and spirit, both modern and primitive.[6]

To use the word "primitive" as a positive adjective is to invite general misunderstanding. "Wild" is a possible synonym but it, too, can be easily misunderstood. "Savage" creates the same problem, as in the images of witless virtue projected by Rousseau's Emile and the term "noble savage." I hope to avoid such misunderstandings by definition: by primitive, I mean a state of affairs in which humans know themselves as part of the natural world. Primitive persons see their inventions and creations, their pots, their clothes, their tools and weapons, their stories and dances, not as artifacts, but as natural extensions of the world.

Primitive human life is responsive to the cycles of nature; of the moon, the tides, the seasons. It is also responsive to the cycles of glut and famine, of birth and death. Primitives know the taste and smell of fear as much as of joy. Their intimacy with the spirits is harmoniously one with their knowledge of matter. A dream experience is as real and legitimate as is a waking one. There is a kind of balance implied in which there is both sickness and healing, sacred and profane, comedy and tragedy, comfort and discomfort. Primitives know that to shirk one or other element of these kinds of couples is to shirk the essence of living. It is this balance that participants can find, I would argue, on canoe trips, more so than anywhere else in our culture.

So-called civilized culture holds an image of itself and its people as separate from the world of nature whether material or spiritual or both. It distances itself from the natural to maximize the pleasant and minimize the unpleasant. Domination and control of nature is a high value. What we can't control, we try to escape. Male children are told, "Big boys don't cry." And, when we are frightened by a dream, the words of comfort are words of denial: "There, there, it wasn't real. It was only a dream. Everything's all right now." Alienation is rampant.

The boy was sixteen. He strolled rhythmically along the street. A closer view showed the ear phones on his head and the dangling wires leading to swinging jacket pocket. He paused at the corner, swaying slightly, waiting, but not waiting. He seemed not to be there.

The bus swung into the street and roared toward the corner. Brakes hissed and doors opened as, glassy-eyed, the boy entered. His eyes shifted and focussed as he fumbled for the fare and muttered. Then he found a seat and was lost again in the mad oblivion of sound in his head. He travelled this same bus each day. So did most of the other passengers. But not one spoke to another. Indeed, not one knew the name of one other. The driver might have identified "the shaky lady at Pine and Maple" or "the kid with the ear phones," only the drivers were rotated from route to route often enough to discourage fraternization and identification with customers.

This is a picture of alienation. Internal alienation goes along with being estranged from the rest of the world around, from the quality of the interior of the bus to the lives of the trees on the streets.

Cartoonist Jim Unger begins his *1980 Annual of Herman* cartoons with these words:

Ever since I was a little kid, I was absolutely convinced the world was crazy.

There I was, a defenceless child, and they had everything completely sewn up before I even got here. They had it all organized and it was utter chaos.

Things really started to get messy when I had to learn the local language. As soon as I was able to understand, they told me I had been assigned a nationality, a race, and a religion. Needless to say they already had a name picked out for me.

I eventually realized I would have to blend in for a few years, so when I got to school I pretended everything made sense. I even learned the words to the school song.[7]

In a less light-hearted tone, alienation of youth in modern culture has been described by others. Kurt Hahn was convinced that the young were in a state of decline. He perceived lack of mental and physical toughness, loss of pride in craftsmanship and, above all, the inability to be compassionate.

Laing[6] not only asserts the fact of alienation, he documents the processes by which the Stone Age infant is relentlessly manoeuvered into this unnatural state which he characterizes as a form of collective madness called "normal sanity." The general process is to deny the experiences of the child and thus to impose "a straight jacket of conformity." For youth, and perhaps others too, canoe tripping loosens the grip of conformist attitudes. In Laing's view, interactions among people, especially between parents and children, consist of negating each other's experiences. In this way, individuals are cut off from the inner spiritual experience. Canoe tripping, as I have seen it with the Trekkers, forges new communication links because of the exigencies of the simpler environment.

From a different perspective, Evernden[8] claims that personal alienation is a function of excessive reliance on Cartesian categories and on the "despotism of the eye" as a way of knowing what's out there. Evernden raises the frightening prospect that humanity may be performing the role of an exotic species in the biosphere and may literally be beyond the normal ecological limitations short of catastrophe.

In contrast to Evernden, whose account of alienation is taken back only as far as Descartes, Diamond[8] traces it back to Plato, who banished the bards from the ideal state. *The Republic*, says Diamond, has influenced western thought to the total displacement of those parts of humanity which promote awareness and unity of the inner and outer worlds. Diamond describes the Renaissance as the time when the individual was discovered and elevated to a status which isolated and eventually alienated. Clearly we have inherited a long tradition of estrangement from each other and the natural world. This estrangement makes it very difficult, if not impossible, to appreciate the primitive and to see the values in primitive views of the world.

Joseph Meeker[10] considers the same questions from the perspective of literary ecology. He shows that our culture has had a long and exclusive love affair with tragedy. The tragic hero is well known to us. The comic hero, or trickster, referred to earlier, is much less well known and admired in our culture, although there are signs that the situation may be changing, as evidenced by behaviour of Mackenzie High School Trekkers and the popularity of trickster cartoon characters. The point is that a culture which holds tragedy to be a higher art form than comedy is incompletely connected to the world. Destructive and death-dealing impulses are more strongly favoured than are the constructive, life-affirming ones.

Thus, writers in the fields of education, psychiatry, literature, anthropology and environmental science have articulated their images of the alienated state of modern civilized humanity. The total picture is dark indeed, and it would be tempting to leave it to despair. However, there are some avenues of hope for rediscovery of relationship that should be explored. The first avenue of hope for many Canadians may well be the wilderness canoe trip.

Native elders are currently active in promoting total relationship for all human beings. The basic position of the elders is that alienation occurs because we fail to teach people how to discover who they are and what is their true path. The discovery of personal identity in relation to humans and earth as kin is a central teaching of the elders. From this identity and kinship one may then learn what is the proper road to follow, and learn the means needed to follow it. The sacredness of relationships, material and spiritual, makes the discovery of one's path in life a sacred learning elevated far beyond the pettiness of career planning.

Related to the increasing influence of the native elders is the modern emergence of comic characters as folk heroes. There is no doubt in my mind that the wildly comic archetype of the trickster is alive and well when high school students travel by canoe. But for now, we should not forget the popularity of cartoon characters like Garfield, Snoopy, Herman and the drawings of Larson ("The Far Side") to support the claim that our cultural need for acquaintance with the trickster is asserting itself.

Unger provides a prose example:

The first two words they teach you when you're a kid are good and bad. They don't explain them fully at the time, but it becomes apparent that when you do something that meets the approval of those around you, you're doing good. Bad means something that those around you find disagreeable. This polarity has nothing whatsoever to do with right or wrong. For exactly the same deed, the same human being can either receive a shiny new medal or face a firing squad, depending where he, or she, gets off the bus. You have to keep your sense of humour.[11]

Barry Lopez, well known explorer and author, describes both the threat of alienation and the antidote he has discovered in his relationship with a river:

I have travelled into the Canadian Arctic, to Japan and southern Africa ... I always come home to this river. By its seethe and purl, the sight of mergansers landing on it, the tug of it against my thighs, I recover some sense of who I am. ...Gradually, over several millenia, we've traded in a fraternal or companionable relationship with the land for an economic one ... the land as a thing. When I return after a journey, I do not find myself wishing only to preserve this river, ... I want to preserve the ground of our relationship. It is founded, for my part, on regard for the mystery inherent in all life ... From this attitude of respect is derived my sense of home, of responsibility to community, and the admonition to lead a dignified and compassionate life.

If we do not retrieve and nurture, I think, some more gracious relationship with the land, we will find our sanctuaries, in the end, have become nothing more than commodities. They will not be the inviolate and healing places we yearn for, but landscapes related to no one.[12]

Educators, too, have felt obliged to counter the increasing alienation of their students and themselves. Kurt Hahn's contribution in this direction persists in the Gordonstoun School, the United World Colleges and the Outward Bound Schools. The latter are most relevant in this context because they use wilderness experiences as the chief tool for reducing the barriers to learning relationship. Outward Bound Schools vary widely in their curricula and in the intensity and purposes of their courses. But they all have in common a high value on validating the experience, past and present, of students, and the establishment of communities of relationship, not only within groups but towards the land.[13]

The canoe trip works to accomplish the sort of things which Kurt Hahn had in mind to counter the physical and spiritual decline in the youth of his day. The natural exigencies of wilderness travel impel everyone to discover the hidden unities of comfort and discomfort, fear and confidence, misery and fun. In Charity James' terms,[14] the canoe trip is dialogue with a river, opening opportunities for wonder, both in the contrasting power and tranquility of the world experienced at first hand, and in the penetration to explore more fully the meaning of that wonder. In philosophical terms, the canoe trip paves the way for a more connected, less exploitive relationship among persons and the world. There are strong trends to say "You" to the world, rather than "It."[15] Canoe trip experiences create the opportunity to feel like Lopez about the earth, to grow beyond the belittling breeding described by Unger and perhaps even to be free to act out comic roles by being a Garfield. That this potential is not fully realized almost goes without saying. But the possibilities are there. They represent potent opportunities to rediscover our lost Stone Age inheritance.

Notes

1   Nash, R. *Wilderness and the American Mind* (Revised edition). New Haven: Yale University Press, 1973.

2   Horwood, B. "Getting Along: Learning About Interpersonal Relationships on a Canoe Trip," *Outdoor Recreation Research Journal* 2, 1987, pp 35-46.

3   Old Man Coyote, an American Indian hero with a thousand faces—and a thousand tricks—is explained very nicely through original native tales in

Lopez, B. *Giving Birth to Thunder, Sleeping with his Daughter: Coyote Builds North America*. New York: Avon Books, 1977.

4 James, T. *Do the Mountains Speak for Themselves?* Denver: Colorado Outward Bound School, 1980.

5 Hubert, C. *Dreamspeaker*. New York: Avon Books, 1981.

6 Laing, R.D. *The Politics of Experience*. Harmondsworth: Penguin Books, 1967.

7 Unger, J. *The Second Herman Treasury*. New York: Andrews, McMeel, and Parker, 1980, p 1.

8 Evernden, N. *The Natural Alien: Humankind and the Environment*. Toronto: University of Toronto Press, 1985.

9 Diamond, S. *In Search of the Primitive: A Critique of Civilization*. New Brunswick, New Jersey: Transaction Books, 1981.

10 Meeker, J. *The Comedy of Survival: In Search of an Environmental Ethic*. Los Angeles: International Guild of Tutors Press, 1980.

11 Unger, p 33.

12 Lopez, B. "Environmental Statement," *Life*, July 1987, p 40.

13 Wilson, R. *Inside Outward Bound: The Success Story of the International Wilderness School*. Vancouver: Douglas and McIntyre, 1981.

14 James, C. *Young Lives at Stake*. London: Collins, 1968.

15 Evernden, p 136.

Hubbard and Wallace: The Rivals

Gwyneth Hoyle

What follows is perhaps one of the greatest Canadian canoe stories of all time. It tells of adventure, starvation, death, struggle with the northern elements of land, weather and water, and bitter rivalry between a man and a woman. It is a story—a well researched and patently true story to be sure—but as such says nothing direct about the canoe in Canadian culture. Rather than being commentary, it is a piece of culture itself. Infused between the lines is an account of the forces that drive people to canoe the wilderness, and a stirring portrait of the inexorable beckoning of a northern river.   EDITORS

Rivalry is a powerful force in all fields of human endeavor. Rivalry fuelled by animosity has an added intensity that can impel those affected to spectacular lengths. Mina Benson Hubbard[1] and Dillon Wallace[2] were such rivals when they set off in 1905 on separate expeditions on the same day from Northwest River in Labrador with the same purpose—to find the George River and follow it to the point where it empties into Ungava Bay. The result of this contest was that Mina Hubbard became not only the first woman, but indeed the first white person to complete this journey of nearly 600 miles through a barren and forbidding wilderness. Dillon Wallace, denied the achievement of being first to finish this race, added to the arduous canoe trip an unprecedented winter journey by snowshoe and dog team along the entire length of the Labrador coast from Fort Chimo to beyond the Quebec border.

The silent protagonist in this drama was Leonidas Hubbard, Mina's husband, a close friend and canoeing partner of Wallace on their ill-fated attempt to find the George River in

1903. The 1903 expedition was dogged by misfortune from the outset. Misinformation from the shipping companies gave them a late start, and inaccurate information sent them up the wrong river, the Susan, to cite just two examples, Disappointed, anxious and homesick, Leonidas Hubbard succumbed to starvation deep in the Labrador bush. Dillon Wallace was rescued through the heroic efforts of the third member of the party, George Elson, the half-breed Cree from Missinaibi, who was their hired guide.

Leonidas Hubbard was a romantic. His favourite author was Kipling, and his most used adjective was "bully," in the style of Theodore Roosevelt. He had learned to fish and shoot as a child in Michigan on his father's farm, close to the frontier, in the 1870s. He graduated from Ann Arbor and broke into journalism on a New York City daily. It was a proud moment when he had one of his wilderness articles accepted by *Atlantic Monthly*. When he was made an assistant editor of *Outing Magazine* he was in his natural element. About this time he married Mina Benson and they settled into a large, handsome house on the edge of the village of Congers, just across the Hudson River, north of New York City. Within easy reach were the Shawangunk Hills, still an unpopulated wilderness area, and a favourite camping area of Hubbard's.

It was on a camping trip in the Shawangunk Hills in November 1901 when they were caught in an early snowfall that Hubbard first suggested the Labrador trip to Dillon Wallace, a New York lawyer, older than himself, who had recently lost his young wife. While Labrador held a fascination for Hubbard as one of the unexplored areas of the continent, he looked on the expedition as a way to make a name for himself as an explorer in his position with *Outing Magazine*.

The editor of *Outing*, Caspar Whitney, well known writer and explorer of the time, did not originally consider Hubbard's proposed trip to Labrador to be of sufficient interest to be worth the time and money. The magazine did, in the end, give its financial support to the expedition although, as Whitney was careful to point out after Hubbard's death, Hubbard had neither consulted nor informed anyone at the magazine about the details of the trip.

Mina Hubbard travelled with her husband and Wallace as far as Battle Harbour on Labrador's south coast when they set off with such high hopes in June of 1903. Her return to Congers to await news of the expedition was an agonizing time for her. The months crawled by as autumn became winter, and still there was no word. Her husband had been dead for three months before the grim telegram arrived, shattering all her hopes. Letters containing the details would be two months longer in arriving. Wallace had prepared the letters and telegrams as soon as he was able, but the nearest cable office was south of Battle Harbour, and the messages would travel out from Northwest River with the regular winter mail courier late in December when it was possible to run a dog team over the 300 miles along the coast.

The few reports in the *New York Times* caused nothing but distress to the grief-stricken widow, hungry for any news. In January, 1904, the *Times* carried a front-page story stating that the members of the expedition were on their way to the coast with Hubbard's body, and would reach there by March, yet in actual fact the body had not been recovered from its snowbound tent deep in the woods. In March, headlines, again on the front page, declared: "*Outing* expedition leader perished—only a few hours walk from food." This damaging report stated that the explorers had cached all their provisions, expecting to live on game, but they had become exhausted after a few days. In retracing their steps, Hubbard's strength failed him, so his companions went on, secured provisions and returned in a few hours to find that he had died. This story made Hubbard appear to be not only very weak, but foolish as well.

More authentic information reached the paper a few days later when Wallace's letter to his sister covered a full column on page one. Wallace's hardships made graphic headlines: "Lost for days in storm, Wallace in stocking feet and underwear, hatless and coatless when rescued—had eaten cowhide mittens." Wallace assured his sister that he was now in perfect health, indeed better than ever before, and his letter glows with vigour and energy, in stark contrast to Hubbard's pathetic death.

When Wallace reached New York with Hubbard's body, the story was no longer front page news. The rigours of the journey were described in glorious detail along with Wallace's splendid good health. The headlines proclaimed that the lack of a fishnet and a shotgun were fatal, and Wallace offered the very odd suggestion that Hubbard was overtrained for the expedition.

It was noted that Mina Hubbard, prostrate with grief, was not at the pier when the ship docked.

Hubbard had requested that, if he did not survive, Wallace should write the story of their expedition. Feeling that it would be a fitting memorial to her husband, Mina Hubbard allowed Wallace to use Hubbard's diary, as well as contributing $1000 to the cost of having it published. The resulting book, *The Lure of Labrador Wild*, appeared early in 1905, and received considerable praise as a tale of hardship bravely endured and movingly told. Mina Hubbard was horrified by the book. The husband she adored was portrayed as weak and sentimental. While the close comradeship between Wallace and Hubbard shines through on every page, the book clearly trumpeted Wallace and diminished Hubbard.

Mina Hubbard became convinced that she must go to Labrador and complete her husband's work so that, if she were successful, the name of Hubbard would be forever connected with it. She was given an assurance of success by George Elson, the guide in the 1903 expedition. In the months that he had spent in Labrador retrieving Hubbard's body, Elson had learned much about the topography of the river systems, and he understood exactly where the fatal mistake had been made.

Dillon Wallace, too, was obsessed with his promise to Hubbard that he would complete the expedition as planned, and this promise was stressed in Wallace's subsequent writings. With this in mind, Wallace kept all of Hubbard's maps, notes and field observations, widening the rift with Mina Hubbard to the point that neither ever spoke to the other again.

Referring to George Elson in his book, Dillon Wallace said, "Once in the wilderness we made no distinctions as to master and servant; we were all companions together." As soon as Elson had effected Wallace's rescue from the winter-bound bush, and Wallace was recuperating from severe frostbite, that companionship was forgotten.

In George Elson, Mina Hubbard found a ready friend and ally. When it became known that *Outing* was preparing to send Dillon Wallace on another expedition to the George River in 1905, Mina Hubbard accepted Elson's offer to guide, and began to organize her own expedition.

Mina Hubbard's resolve to vindicate her husband was stiffened when *Outing*, in a special edition in tribute to him, in

March 1905, published his diary in full, with all the details she wished kept private. In his foreword to the article, Caspar Whitney writes of Hubbard "as brave and gentle and lovable a soul as ever breathed in human form" but, at the same time, he pointedly dissociated himself from the fatal expedition.

Mina Hubbard was a woman of spirit. Born in 1870, in the small village of Bewdley, Ontario, on Rice Lake, she had gone to Brooklyn, New York, to train as a nurse in the 1890s when most young women would not have ventured so far from home. Her ambition was rewarded and she advanced rapidly in the profession to become nursing superintendent of a hospital in Richmond, Virginia. Having married Leonidas Hubbard in 1901, she travelled with him on a canoe trip north of Lake Superior, and thus had some familiarity with wilderness travel.

Recognizing the mistakes of the previous expedition, Mina Hubbard planned with meticulous care, providing food in sufficient quantity to ensure that they would not be dependent on rod and gun. She included good camping equipment. And to ensure that Leonidas Hubbard's exploration objectives could be achieved, she included the most up-to-date devices to measure geographical locations and climate.

In contrast, writing about his choice of crew, Wallace makes an oblique disclaimer of Mina Hubbard's eventual success:

I might with one canoe and one or two professional Indian packers travel more rapidly than with men unused to exploration work, but in that case scientific research would have to be slighted. I therefore decided to sacrifice speed to thoroughness and to take with me men who, even though they might not be physically able to carry the large packs of the professional voyageur, would in other respects lend valuable assistance to the work in hand.[3]

Taking two canoes, he chose two students, George Richards, a geologist, and Clifford Easton, a forester; Leigh Stanton, a Nova Scotian Boer War veteran and lumberjack; and an Ojibway Indian from Minnesota who would serve as woodsman, hunter and camp servant.

Northwest River was little more than a trading post at the far end of Hamilton Inlet, and to reach it required some ingenuity. Wallace and his party sailed from New York to St. John's on May 30 and were delayed there waiting until June 15 for the coastal mail boat to Rigolet. Arriving there after midnight in fog, Wallace was delighted to find a steamer en route from Nova Scotia to Kenemish, the trading post opposite Northwest River. They quickly transferred their outfit to the *Harlow*, expecting to sail at daybreak. Already on board, having sailed from Halifax on June 16, was Mina Hubbard and her party! This may explain Wallace's haste on arrival at Kenemish in thunder, drenching rain and pitch darkness, in sending his crew immediately to canoe the 12 miles across to the Hudson's Bay post at Northwest River, while he followed with the bulk of the luggage in a trapper's boat. At 2:00 a.m., soaked to the skin, it was an emotional homecoming for Wallace to arrive at the post where he had spent five months recuperating the year before.

The Hubbard party remained at the French trading post at Kenemish until Monday morning, June 26, when they crossed to Northwest River to make the final assemblage of their outfit. Both Hubbard and Wallace were sincere Christians and would not have involved anyone in the work of preparation on the Sabbath, hence the delay. Wallace left Northwest River first thing Monday morning to paddle three miles up to the rapid at the beginning of Grand Lake.

For Hubbard, the packing continued until noon the next day. At 3:15 p.m., June 27—just one day later than Wallace—Mina Hubbard was launched in the waters she hoped would carry her to Ungava Bay in time to board the only ship of the year that would call at the mouth of the George River.

From the beginning, Wallace made slow progress. The young men were interested in stopping to hunt and to collect geological specimens, crossing and recrossing the lake. By sunset they had made 20 miles and were camped on the north shore by Watty's Brook, and Wallace was in a mood to remember:

As I sat that night by the low-burning embers of our first campfire I forgot my new companions. Through the gathering night mists I could just discern the dim outlines of the opposite shore of Grand Lake. It was over there, just west of that high spectral bluff that Hubbard and I, on a wet July night two years before, had pitched our first camp of the other trip. ... In fancy I was back again in that camp and Hubbard was talking to me and telling me of the "bully story" of the mystic land of wonders that lay behind the ranges he would have to take back to the world.[4]

While he sat nursing his memories, Mina Hubbard had touched the opposite shore to make a brief first camp. To make up for their late start, George Elson had pushed the canoes on until 11:00 p.m., and by 3:00 the next morning they were away up the lake, entering the Nascaupee River by 8:00 a.m. Wallace camped again only three miles up the Nascaupee. Hubbard had more than made up for Wallace's head start of 24 hours.

Thirteen miles up the Nascaupee River, a decision had to be made on the route ahead. An old Indian portage left the river and made its way overland through a series of small lakes to Seal Lake, the first flat water on the Nascaupee. According to the trappers at Northwest River, it would take a month to reach Seal Lake travelling up the river, but the Indians were known to reach Seal Lake in two weeks by the portage route. The Indians at Northwest River had provided both Hubbard and Wallace with crude maps of the portage route. George Elson knew what it was like to try to find the way through a confusing tangle of unknown Labrador lakes, and Mina Hubbard wished very much to go by the river route because that was the way her husband would have gone had he not missed the way. They made the decision to stay with the river despite the slow progress against the strong current and the heavy rapids.

Wallace declared that his object was to trace the old Indian trail and explore as much of the country as possible, and not to hide himself in an enclosed river valley.

Neither route was easy. The Hubbard party poled up rapids and strong currents, and portaged around rapids too long and heavy to be navigable. Progress was discouragingly slow, at times as little as one and a half miles a day. The portage route proved to be no better. It had to be be searched out and cleared at each small lake, sometimes a day or more being given up to the search. Portaging over heights of land in the blazing sun, under the constant assault of mosquitoes and black flies tested the mettle of the tenderfoot members of Wallace's crew. They reached Seal Lake on August 4. The Hubbard party had passed through Seal Lake on July 15. In such virgin country the smallest signs of other travellers would not have escaped the watchful eyes of George Elson and his crew. Mina Hubbard wrote:

I had seen not only Seal Lake, I had seen the Nascaupee River flowing out of it. ... best of all, there came the full realization that I was first in the field, and the honor of exploring the Nascaupee and the George Rivers was to fall to me.[5]

After Seal Lake, the hardest part of the trip was over for Mina Hubbard. She had come to terms with the over-protectiveness of George Elson and his men, and they in turn had come to accept her, joking and teasing her, even though they spoke among themselves mainly in Cree. While they were still moving slowly upstream against the current, the portages were fewer and the scenery more beautiful. Mina Hubbard, from her seat in the canoe, was free to make observations and write impressions of what she saw:

The trip was proving so beautiful and easy that my state of mind was one of continual surprise. I had none of the feeling of loneliness which I knew everyone would expect me to have. I did not feel far from home but, in reality, less homeless than I had ever felt anywhere since I knew my husband was never to come back to me. So far I had encountered none of the real stress of wilderness life, everything had gone well with us, everything was made easy for me; I had had no hardships to bear and there was the relief of work to do, work which would forever associate my husband's name with country where he had hoped to begin his exploration. For long months of darkness I had not dreamed that I could ever have the gladness and honor of doing this. Now it seemed I might almost count on success.[6]

In contrast to Mina Hubbard's wilderness experience, Wallace wrote, as they were approaching Seal Lake:

The day was one of the most trying ones of the trip, and the men with hands and faces swollen, bleeding from the attacks of not only the small black flies which were particularly bad, but also the swarms of "bulldogs," complained bitterly of the hardships.[7]

Their spirits could rise as quickly when they were spared the labour of portaging and were afloat on a stream so they could lift their eyes to enjoy the rugged beauty, or when good fishing or a patch of wild berries supplemented their diminishing supplies and they had a good meal.

About fifty miles up the Nascaupee from Seal Lake, the Indian portage route began again, foreshadowing another long stretch of rough water. The Hubbard expedition chose to keep to the river as far as possible, finding their own portage route where necessary. Wallace, in camp with a slight injury, sent some of the others ahead to scout the Indian route, and considered whether they should abandon the attempt to find it and follow the river which was beyond doubt the quicker and easier route. But, says Wallace in his book, "My inclinations rebelled against this course. One of the things that Hubbard had planned to do, was to locate the old trail if possible. To abandon the search for it now, and to follow the easier route seemed to me a surrender."[8]

The next important landmark was Lake Michikamau, the large body of water which marked the end of the upstream struggle on the Nascaupee. This was the touchstone for which Leonidas Hubbard had searched so desperately. When he finally came within sight of it after a 40-mile portage, the season was too far advanced, and their supplies were so depleted that, after being storm-stayed for nearly a week on Lake Windbound, he made the painful decision to turn back and retrace their steps over the tortuous trail they had come.

It was a very emotional moment for the leaders of both expeditions when they finally reached Lake Michikamau, Mina Hubbard on August 2, and Dillon Wallace a month later, on September 3. Leonidas Hubbard had not actually reached the lake—he had viewed it with George Elson from the mountain which now bears his name and which Elson pointed out to Mina Hubbard, only a few miles from where they were standing. As she wrote later, "the whole desperate picture stood out with dreadful vividness."[9]

For Wallace, the sight was equally poignant:

I cannot describe my emotions. I was living over again that beautiful September day two years before when Hubbard had told me with so much joy that he had seen the big lake—that Michikamau lay just beyond the ridge. Now I was on its very shores—the shores of the lake that we had so longed to reach. How well I remembered those weary, wind-bound days and the awful weeks that followed.[10]

Once they had reached the height of land on August 10, the main concern for Mina Hubbard was whether they now had sufficient time to reach the mouth of the George River in time to catch the only ship of the season, due there before the end of the month. For several days, they witnessed the spectacle when the country for fifty miles around was alive with migrating caribou. By the time she wrote her book, Mina Hubbard knew that she was the only white person to have seen the great migration in the interior of Labrador, just as she knew when she stood on the summit of the Divide that she was the first white person to trace the Nascaupee River to its source. Along the George River they met encampments of both Montagnais and the more isolated Nascaupee Indians. Her descent of the George River was swift and her arrival at the Hudson's Bay post at the mouth on August 27 was triumphant.

To reach Lake Michikamau, Dillon Wallace and his party had made camp 46 times, had cut and double-carried many portages, taking 70 days to achieve 325 miles. The food pack was depleted, the weather was turning colder, and Wallace made the decision which had been forecast in New York. The trip would be completed with one canoe and one companion; the other three would return to Northwest River. Before they reached the end of the trail, Wallace and Easton would narrowly escape death twice.

Despite the lateness of the season, Wallace and Easton proceeded slowly, spending a day with an encampment of Montagnais near the beginning of the George River on September 16. The caribou migration had passed but, soon after leaving the Indians, they shot two caribou and spent four days caching much of the meat in case of the need to turn back. The hunger for animal fat caused them to overindulge, and two more days were spent recuperating. It was September 29 when they launched the canoe again in a blinding snowstorm. As the storm abated, the air became colder; the spray froze on their clothing, the canoe and paddles became weighted with ice, and the accident happened. The canoe hit a submerged rock, swung around in the current, and tipped them into the icy water. Wallace's incredible will to survive pulled them through when death from hypothermia was imminent. Their heavy packs were lost but fortunately, canoe, paddles, clothing, tent, and 50 pounds of pemmican, tallow and tea came to rest downstream in an eddy where it could be salvaged. Guns, ammunition, axes, cooking pots and the bulk of their provisions were gone.

There were no further accidents, but with the Labrador winter closing in as they travelled north to meet it, and the loss of much of their outfit, there was little comfort in their

campsites as they travelled down the river that had become almost a continuous rapid:

The wilderness gripped us closer and closer as the days went by.
Remembrances of the outside world were becoming like dream-land
fancies. ... It seemed to us that all our lives we had been going on and
on through rushing water or with packs over rocky portages, and the
Post we were aiming to reach appeared no nearer to us than it did the
day we left Northwest River—long, long ago. We seldom spoke.
Sometimes in a whole day not a dozen words would be exchanged.[11]

It was October 16 when they reached tidewater, and night
was falling when they came in sight of the post, unattainable
across the wide expanse of tidal mud. Late in the evening, they
were rescued and conducted to the agent's house where white
bread and jam, served at a table, on a tablecloth, seemed a feast.
That night, listening to the wind and rain from the snug warmth
of feather beds and blankets, should have been the epitome of
luxury. Wallace claimed that four months of sleeping in a tent
on spruce boughs made him claustrophobic in a house. There

was some truth in this, but his real discomfort lay in finding that Mina Hubbard was also a guest in the house, still waiting for the ship which had not arrived.

The navigation season was almost over so far north, and everyone feared that the once-a-year ship would not be coming. The Hubbard party of five, bringing with them 150 pounds of surplus food, was welcomed with true northern hospitality. Wallace, anxious not to impose himself further on the good will of the Hudson's Bay post, proposed engaging an Eskimo with a boat to take him around the coast to the larger post at Fort Chimo. No Eskimo from George River was willing to risk the journey, and Wallace prepared to wait it out at the post, in the company of Mina Hubbard, until he could travel overland by dog team.

Three days after their arrival at the post, a commotion at the wharf announced the arrival of the *Pelican*, the overdue supply ship, along with Eskimo pilots. The Eskimos reported large herds of caribou heading toward the Koksoak River which flows out at Fort Chimo. Wallace proclaimed his wish to see these herds as reason for not wishing to return south on the *Pelican*. Wallace would have used any excuse not to be confined in the small coastal steamer with Mina Hubbard, who had successfully completed the exploration of the Nascaupee and George Rivers in record time.

As the *Pelican* steamed out of George River on October 22, carrying Mina Hubbard south to reach New York by the end of November, a second boat, with Wallace, Easton, and a crew of three non-English-speaking Eskimos, set off along the coast of Ungava Bay back to Fort Chimo. Wallace and Easton were still wearing the ravaged clothing they had worn throughout the Labrador summer, having left the George River post in too much haste to re-equip themselves from the newly arrived supplies. They had with them provisions for ten days, but the Eskimos had only a bag of hard-tack biscuits. Their boat was suddenly frozen in only five days after, and they were forced to start on foot for Whale River where there was a small Hudson's Bay post. After three days of plodding through the snow, building igloos to camp, and with limited rations, Wallace and Easton could go no further. They were left in a log shack with a rifle while the Eskimos went on through the raging snowstorm to find help. It was six days before a rescue party reached them, and they later learned that their Eskimo companions had almost succumbed to the storm and starvation.

Wallace finally reached Fort Chimo to find that the caribou had passed but, undaunted and outfitted with new winter gear, he was impatient to be off again on the long trek down the coast, despite the generous hospitality of the Hudson's Bay Company. When the Eskimos arrived for the Christmas festivities, he was able to arrange for two men with a dog team to take them on the first leg of the journey home.

Two months later, after struggling through blizzards in sub-zero temperatures, over sea inlets rough with tidal ice ridges, after cajoling and begging native Labradorians to leave their shelters and transport them by dog team each leg of the journey, and after sharing igloos, Moravian mission homes and various shacks, Wallace and Easton reached Northwest River, where they continued south to the Quebec shore of the St. Lawrence and thence to New York, arriving on April 30.

Back in New York, the rivalry between Mrs. Hubbard and Dillon Wallace continued. The ship which brought Mina Hubbard from Ungava also brought letters from Wallace. When the *New York Times* carried an account of the successful conclusion of both George River expeditions on November 23, Wallace with his buoyant optimism and dashing style captured the main headlines and two-thirds of the article. While it was noted that Mina Hubbard was first to achieve their common goal, Wallace was given the credit for being the first white man to cross Labrador without an Indian guide.

Then came the race to publish. Mina Hubbard, with her advantage of an early return to New York, had an account of her journey published by *Harper's Monthly* in May, 1906. More significant was the article which was published in the bulletin of the American Geographical Society later that year, giving to her achievement the recognition of an important scientific body.

Dillon Wallace, sponsored by *Outing*, had a publisher ready and waiting for him. The serialized story of his adventure ran in that magazine for almost a year beginning in August 1906, and was published with little alteration as *The Long Labrador Trail* shortly after the serial finished. Caspar Whitney, in his foreword to the series, praised Wallace's story as "not only a virile and absorbing narrative of the great outdoors but also a splendid record of American courage, endurance

and heroism." Other reviewers praised the book but with less
enthusiasm, finding that the roughness of the prose matched the
grim determination of the undertaking.

Mina Hubbard's book, *A Woman's Way Through Unknown Labrador* did not appear in New York until 1908. The
book contained not only her own story, but also a carefully edited
version of the diary of Leonidas Hubbard, portraying him in the
best possible light, and George Elson's journal of part of the
earlier Hubbard trip. Her book also included a first-rate map
of the Nascaupee and George rivers, with details of camp sites,
portages and descriptions of the landforms, contributed by the
American Geographical Society, and far superior to the sketch
map which Wallace had included in *The Long Labrador Trail.*
While her prose was restrained and descriptive, the prefaces to
the book allude to the criticism of her husband which led her to
undertake the expedition, and to the fact that she had never
been given access to his maps or field notes. Her book was given
a mixed reception by reviewers. Some praised it with great
warmth, others criticized the presentation and lack of scientific
value, comparing it unfavorably to Wallace's *Lure of Labrador
Wild*, deprecating her for slighting Wallace's services to her
husband.

With the publication of her book, Mina Hubbard felt that
she had completed the work her husband had set out to do, and
had assured that his name would be forever connected with the
exploration of Labrador.

Dillon Wallace, in his two Labrador expeditions, discovered that his true vocation was bound up in the wilderness. He
became a prolific writer of adventure books for boys, opened a
boys' camp in Wyoming, and gave up his law practice. He remained faithful to the memory of his great friend Leonidas
Hubbard, returning in 1913 to the scene of Hubbard's death
with a bronze tablet to be placed on the rock which stood in front
of the tent site. On the trip, the canoe was submerged in rapids,
the plaque was lost, and a chiselled inscription had to be impro-
vised.

Leonidas Hubbard, the gentle, wilderness romantic, in his
gallant but pathetic struggle in the Labrador wilds, is remembered partly because of his wife's resolutely efficient journey in
the care of George Elson, and partly because of the blundering
energy of Dillon Wallace's epic tale of survival. More important

in keeping his story alive is the tension created by the furious rivalry between the two. Without this impetus, the memory of Leonidas Hubbard would long ago have faded to obscurity. The outpouring of human emotions cloaked in genteel silence which characterized that rivalry adds a dimension which raises the story above that of an ordinary wilderness adventure, and assures that it continues to be retold nearly a century later.

Notes

1 Hubbard, M. B. *A Woman's Way Through Unknown Labrador*. London: Murray, 1908.

2 Wallace, D.. *Lure of the Labrador Wild*. New York: Revell, 1905.

3 Wallace, D. *The Long Labrador Trail*. New York: Outing Publishing Co., 1907, p 4.

4   Wallace, *Labrador Trail*, p 14.

5 Hubbard, p 107.

6 Hubbard, pp 107-15.

7 Wallace, *Labrador Trail*, p 77.

8 Wallace, *Labrador Trail*, p 90.

9 Hubbard, p 139.

10 Wallace, *Labrador Trail*, p 117.

11 Wallace, *Labrador Trail*, p 126.

Solitude and Kinship in the Canoeing Experience

George J. Luste

Any personal experience is difficult to capture in words, and wilderness canoeing is no exception. It is a totally absorbing physical, intellectual, emotional and spiritual experience. Of these, the most difficult to describe clearly are the emotional and spiritual elements and they, of course, are the most personal. In this context the canoe plays a supportive role. It provides the conveyance for the wilderness experience and may contribute to that experience to some degree, but it is not an end in itself.

Why are individuals from all walks of life genuinely and intensely attracted by the wilderness of northern Canada? Why do they go north in the first place? Why do they canoe hundreds of miles, seeking out the wild, sparsely populated corners of the northern landscape? Why do they return or yearn to return long after the initial adventure is only a fading memory?

Surely the basis of a meaningful answer must be more substantive than simple physical enjoyment or intellectual curiosity. My belief is that the strongest personal attraction arises from the emotional and spiritual kinship of the individual with the landscape. (Although this statement seems to imply a distinction between "emotional" and "spiritual," they are in some sense synonyms, referring to the same personal experience in much of the discussion that follows.)

The beckoning curiosity for the new, unseen landscape beyond the immediate horizon is undeniable. So is the possibility of adventure into the unknown, with its real though often exaggerated dangers. Taking a new step, uttering a new word is what people fear most, according to Dostoyevsky, and it often takes some critical, personal decision to make that first step and decide to get out, to do something new. Thinking back nearly thirty years before I had started canoeing, I can vividly recall a moonlit summer night when I was strolling barefoot and alone along a sand beach of the south shore of the Ottawa River. Preoccupied with my thoughts, I happened to glance northward. It must have been past midnight, and the black outlines of the trees on the far shore of the wide river were barely discernible in the darkness. Even now it seems like yesterday, and I can remember the feel of the cool, granular sand under my feet as I stood there transfixed. Then and there I had an overwhelming urge to go and see that "unknown darkness" of the north country. The next day I was planning my first solo canoe trip to James Bay.

The lasting effect of that first solitary northern sojourn was that it introduced me to the gentle rhythms of the natural world. It awakened far deeper emotions and awarenesses than I could have anticipated; some hitherto dormant but basic resonance within had been nudged. The experiences that affected me were both simple and profound. They were truly simple—happenings such as observing the tranquil magic of the early morning light at daybreak—or the stillness of the forest at midday—or the haunting call of the loon at dusk. And enveloping all was the overwhelming presence and immense solitude of the northern landscape itself.

At the time I don't think I was fully conscious of a deeper significance to my canoe venture. It was only years later, after reading the thoughtful prose of others, and reflecting on the meaning of my own experience, that I began to grasp the more substantial complexities. This enriching comprehension of the profundity of those experiences continues to grow to this day. One learns that even the basic notions of wilderness and solitude can be complicated concepts, related to our own perceptions, part and parcel of our emotional and spiritual make-up. The following brief thoughts by the American geographer Yi-Fu Tuan on wilderness and solitude illustrate this enriching interdependence between experience and awareness:

Wilderness cannot be defined objectively, it is as much a state of mind as a description of nature.[1]

Solitude is a condition for acquiring a sense of immensity. Alone, one's thoughts wander freely over space. In the presence of others they are pulled back by an awareness of other personalities who project their own worlds onto the same area. Fear of space often goes with fear of solitude.[2]

Both quotes articulate insights on the intrinsic relationship between the perceiver and the perceived—we project our thoughts and emotions on the wilderness landscape and the landscape in turn mirrors our own psychological landscape. This theme of the relationship between the arctic wilderness and the human psyche is eloquently explored by Barry Lopez in the "Country of the Mind" chapter of his acclaimed book, *Arctic Dreams*:

To inquire into the intricacies of a distant landscape is to provoke thoughts about one's own interior landscape, and the familiar landscape of memory. The land urges us to come around to an understanding of ourselves.[3]

But a canoe trip isn't all sunsets and inspiration. There is, of course, the reality of the physical experience. Wilderness canoeing may exact gut-wrenching work. To push a canoe for a mile on a flat lake may demand 600 paddle strokes. This is easy enough on a calm day, at a leisurely pace, but with an uncooperative wind, a chilly drizzle, a heavily laden canoe and a 30-mile lake with no trees or shelter, one has an unavoidable and exhausting challenge. The feet, inactive and numb with cold, may lose all sensation and behave like foreign stumps appended to the body. The back aches after a long day of hard levering on the paddle, and flashes of pain stab between the shoulder blades. The portage, started too late in the day, mired in an endless bog, tests the most determined resolve with each difficult, sucking step. The black flies, thick as smoke, crawling and searching for exposed flesh under the sweaty canoe on the hot trail, drive one to despair. All these and more are the necessary dues one pays on the journey to the interior landscape of the far north. Quality exacts its price.

But, to turn back to the earlier question: why was I impelled to go north in the first place, and why do I keep going back now? Why?

To attempt an answer I must turn to those emotional and spiritual queries of our youth when we first perceive the mystery of existence, sense our own insignificance and ask: Who am I? Why am I here? How do I find meaning and purpose in my life?

At one time or another we all probably sought answers to these ancient mysteries and, naively, we all may have expected to discover the absolute answer and the reassurance that comes with it. Yet our reason also cautioned us that there would not be any absolutes, there could not be, unless we should be inclined to accept some supreme authority as an *a priori* given. Some accept such authority; others cannot. In this sense my initial encounter with the wilderness was more a reflection of a state of mind and emotional unrest rather than a physical experience.

Albert Einstein, a remarkable scientist and a respected humanitarian, once wrote: "We are here for a brief sojourn, for what purpose we know not, though we sometimes think we feel it." It is just those rare "sometimes" moments of emotional knowing and spiritual kinship that I have experienced most intensely when deep in the natural world of our northern wilderness. Such special moments of emotional awareness can occur while watching the early morning mist of sunrise in the birth of a new day or during the last afterglow of a slow sunset at the close, or at any number of similar instances in between. During those moments, we may feel the answer to this over-whelming question of Why? It is experienced, not with ana-lytical thought but emotionally and spiritually with our whole being. The memory of such special moments, their sense of tranquility, gladness and spiritual healing, lasts forever. Freeman Patterson, the acclaimed Canadian photographer, de-scribes it well:

It's a moment of total, personal immersion in the world around me—a depth of involvement that produces a sense of oneness with Earth itself.[4]

One cannot expect that every personal experience will have universal acceptance, understanding or interpretation. For some individuals this personal affinity to the north is real and compelling, but others may smile and call it fiction, an invention of an overly romantic imagination, or dismiss it as a rational-ization and escapism from our unhappy reality. Yet a number of sensitive individuals, from the earliest times up to present, have expressed the same or similar sentiment.

At the end of the last century, J.B. Tyrrell and his brother James explored the vast open regions of the barren lands for the Geological Survey of Canada. They, like most of their Victorian contemporaries, were private men; they were not prone to public expressions of personal emotion. Yet they did not always totally suppress their personal views. In May of 1893, while visiting the World's Fair in Chicago, en route to Edmonton and his epic Dubawnt River traverse of the barrens, J.B. Tyrrell wrote to his fiancée, Edith:

A crowd of people in a city wearies me beyond endurance, and though the northern life is very lonely, there are none but the powers of Nature to struggle with. The Fair has not left much impression on me.[5]

This sharp contrast of cities and crowds with the quiet wilderness is a common theme. To some, the urban landscape—that ant hill of humanity with its commerce and materialism, where extreme poverty and affluence are cheek by jowl—is found wearisome and wanting whereas, in compelling contrast, the simplicity and beauty of the northern landscape (or similar wilderness setting) has intrinsic appeal.

Elliott Merrick, in the introduction to his 1933 book *True North*, gives a more earnest but similar voice to the estrangement and disaffection one can experience in our urban society. His initial, cutting words at the start of the preface set the tone:

Each June from the educational grist mills come thousands of sad young men who do not take to the great American religion of business, who dislike being sandwich men with signs on their backs that read, "My life is for sale to the highest bidder." They are malcontents who do not know what they want, but they know they do not want to devote their lives to business success with the wholeheartedness necessary to achieve that aim.[6]

Later in the same introduction Merrick continues:

One muggy night just before a thunderstorm, I sat up in bed and hammered my fist on the wall and screamed in my mind, "I'm getting out." And I got out.[7]

This was his moment of decision. To "get out," he left New York and went to Labrador for two and a half years, living in Northwest River near present day Goose Bay and travelling with local trappers up the Grand River into the heart of the

Labrador peninsula. Shortly after his return south (to a small farm in northern Vermont) *True North* was published—a personal and interesting account of his northern experience. It speaks from the heart and rings true, without the sophistry and affectation that can accompany too much formal education. The closing words in the book again turn to the lasting and deeply felt emotional and spiritual kinship he experienced in his northern home:

And a feeling of gladness and sorrow comes over the water to us like a wave; gladness that the earth is so free and wide and life-giving and generous; sorrow that so many millions of men are unhappy, neither knowing nor caring for these things.[8]

A similar fusion of gladness and sorrow greets every receptive soul that seeks beauty and a deeper kinship in the isolated sanctuaries on the earth. Does it really matter if some call this search an escape or therapy or a religious quest? It seems to me that they all speak to the same human longing, a search for meaning and, with it, personal happiness.

As a footnote, it is interesting to muse or speculate on why Merrick did not stay in the north. He does not say. One wonders if he too was trapped between the two worlds, the primitive and the modern, unable to choose one to the permanent exclusion of the other. In this sense, his 30-month stay in the north is akin to our four-week canoe ventures into the interior every summer, and to the periodic return back to the land by the natives themselves in today's northern villages. The interior of that northern landscape has a close bond with the interior of the personal landscape of the human spirit, yet somehow it is difficult to examine that bond too closely or to describe it fully. But it's there; I have glimpsed it. It is personal, it is significant, it is elusive, and capturing it in words is not easily done. "You point to something as having quality and the quality tends to go away," to use Robert Pirsig's words in *Zen and the Art of Motorcycle Maintenance*.

Solitude seems to assume the aura of a metaphor. It is a recurring theme in descriptions of the wilderness and one's experiences in it. We are born alone and we will die alone, but few are inclined to live their days alone in isolation. Yet, to plumb the depths of one's own being, one must travel alone and embrace solitude; only then can we re-experience the sense of oneness with Earth that too often eludes us in the everyday bustle of life. Individuals from all sorts of civilizations, in all sorts of circumstances, have repeated this refrain. The following series of quotes reinforces this claim:

To me a town is like a prison, and the desert loneliness a paradise.[9]

All true wisdom is only found far from the dwellings of men, in the great solitudes; and it can only be attained through suffering. Suffering and privation are the only things that can open the mind of man to that which is hidden from his fellows.[10]

The first great thing is to find yourself and for that you need solitude and contemplation ... or at least sometimes. I tell you, deliverance will not come from the noisy centres of civilization. It will come from the lonely places.[11]

In open space one can become intensely aware of a remembered place; and in the solitude of a sheltered place, the vastness of space acquires a haunting presence.[12]

What exactly is this "remembered place" that Yi-Fu Tuan refers to in this last quote? Like most inspired phrases, it may suggest more to the reader than was intended by the writer. Perhaps this remembered place is the source of our metaphysical or emotional kinship with Earth—that spiritual recognition and sense of oneness. Maybe the remembered place even predates our own births and goes back to a time when people lived closer to the natural world and experienced it intimately on a daily basis. Such personal experiences of kinship with the landscape are not unique to the wilderness canoeist or to the far north; similar observations are echoed by others, such as mountaineers, wanderers of the deserts, or sailors of the oceans. They all seek similar open spaces of land, air, sand or water, and the solitude that can only be found in such empty quarters. In their moments of sensitivity they share a common perception and a deep affinity with that primordial element around us, the natural world from which we have only recently emerged and today too often abuse or ignore. In revisiting those remembered places, our emotional and spiritual roots, our mysterious and troubled inner spirits are soothed and healed.

But these are memories of ancestral roots from our own species, and memories of terrestrial spaces from our own familiar planet. Might this same awareness of a remembered place prevail when confronted with the vast empty reaches of outer space? Would the space traveller in *2001: A Space Odyssey* sense this same familiar remembered place while gazing into the vast empty void of outer space, as does the canoeist who stands all alone on a sandy esker deep in the barren lands? I wonder. Are the starship and the canoe on the same voyage into the interior landscape of the human psyche? (What an intriguing title for a book![13]) Or is the umbilical chord of memory and remembered place too remote to reach back to the cosmic dust of our origins?

It seems fitting to conclude with the erudite wisdom of Najagneq, an Inuk *angakoq* (shaman) in Alaska, who spoke the following powerful words to Rasmussen. With authority derived from profound cognition and mysticism he reaches us across the vast abyss of time and culture and confronts us with this spiritual insight:

I have searched in the darkness, being silent in the great lonely stillness of the dark. ... The ancients devoted their lives to maintaining the balance of the universe; to great things, immense, unfathomable things. ... (I believe in) ... a power we call Sila, which is not to be explained in simple words. A great spirit, supporting the world and the weather and all life on earth, a spirit so mighty that his utterance to mankind is not through common words, but by storm and snow and rain and the fury of the sea; all the forces of nature that men fear. ...When all is well, Sila sends no messages to mankind, but withdraws into his own endless nothingness, apart. So he remains as long as men do not abuse life, but act with reverence towards their daily food. No one has seen Sila; his place of being is a mystery, in that he is at once among us and unspeakably far away.[13]

Notes

1 Tuan, Y. *Topophilia: A Study of Environmental Perception, Attitudes and Values.* Englewood Cliffs, N.J., Prentice-Hall, 1974, p 111.

2 Tuan, Y. *Space and Place: A Perspective of Experience.* Minneapolis: University of Minnesota Press, 1977, p 59.

3 Lopez, B. *Arctic Dreams: Imagination and Desire in a Northern Landscape.* New York: Bantam Books, 1987, p 221.

4 Patterson, F. *Portraits of the Earth*. Toronto: Key Porter Books, 1987, p 7.

5 Tyrrell, E. *I Was There*. Toronto: Ryerson Press, 1938, p 52.

6 Merrick, E. *True North*. New York: Charles Scribner and Sons, 1933, p 3.

7 Merrick, p 6.

8 Merrick, p 353.

9 Words of St. Jerome, ca. A.D.347- 419.

10 Spoken by Igjugarjuk, the Caribou Eskimo living near the Kazan River of northern Canada, as recorded by Knud Rasmussen, the Danish explorer and anthropologist. In Rasmussen, K. *Across Arctic America*. New York: Putnam Publishers, 1927, p 381.

11 Fridtjof Nansen quoted in Simpson, M. *White Horizon*. London: The Travel Book Club, 1967, p 3.

12 Tuan, *Space and Place*, p 54.

13 Brower, K. *The Starship and the Canoe*. London: Whizzard Press, 1978.

14 Rasmussen, p 385.

Of Canoes and Constitutions: Paddling on Meech Lake

Roderick A. Macdonald

In the autumn of 1974 I took three decisions which shaped my life: I married; I enrolled in an LL.M. program hoping to seek a teaching position in law; and I told Kirk Wipper, Director of Camp Kandalore (where I had spent the previous 17 summers), that I would not be returning for an 18th. I need not dwell on the importance of the first. But the other two were equally significant. Abruptly my extra-marital affairs changed from paddling to pleading; from negotiating rapids to negotiating contracts; from teaching a 60-second shakeout to teaching a bankruptcy "workout;" in brief, from canoes to constitutions.

There is a great deal that differentiates the canoe experience from legal experience, but how are they similar? I answer this question by taking two of the fundamental antinomies of modern law and plotting these onto my life with the canoe. From this exercise of reverse mapping I hope to illustrate how the canoe has shaped my current conception of the law, and how it continues to exercise a powerful hold on my own legal imagination.

Let me enter a couple of caveats at the outset. First, it is impossible to know what one's own philosophy of law (or, for that matter, of canoeing) really is. As others have noted, "a philosophy is a point of view, a way of seeing and valuing things, which has meaning that emerges only when compared with other ways of seeing and valuing things." An adequate account of philosophy would, therefore, have to take into consideration all other possible points of view on the same subject. Moreover, the attempt to describe one's own point of view—itself constantly in flux as the ideas which sustain it are accentuated or abandoned—must necessarily be incomplete. I leave it to the reader to fill in the unstated alternative perspectives against which my viewpoint is to be judged, and to supply the implied premises upon which the following analysis rests.

A second caveat issues from the powerful continuity of the self. To believe in the integrity and continuity of oneself is to seek satisfactory explanations over time for one's current beliefs and activities. It is to consider one's personal history as an inexorable progression to the present. Of course, in the late 20th century, scientific or rational notions such as self-knowledge, self-actualization and integration have replaced magical or irrational ideas of nemesis, fate and predestination in the lexicon of personal continuity. But whether characterized as magic or science, the drive for self-continuity remains as strong a feature of human striving today as previously. Hence, whether or not the canoe is a source allegory for the view of the law I am about to present as my own, is quite beside the point. That I believe the canoe serves this function is what matters.

One of my earliest (and most vivid) memories of the canoe was Perry's little manual *The Canoe and You*.[1] In my very first week at Camp Kandalore I had the misfortune of having last choice for sixth period activity on a rainy day. All the good rainy day programs—crafts, ball hockey, rifle cleaning, frog derby—were taken, so I was stuck with canoeing. In 1958, rainy day canoeing consisted of a quick tour of the half-dozen relics Kirk stored in the rafters of the dining hall, plus a memory lesson on types of paddle, parts of the canoe and strokes. Only with the greatest of difficulty did this little ten-year-old manage to learn the difference between draw, pry, bow stroke, C-stroke, J-stroke, front and reverse sweep. Being even then a slightly perverse type, I insisted on knowing what these various strokes were good for. After a quick but unhelpful consultation with Perry, the designated leader (who was also doing sixth period penance with rainy day canoeing) threw me the book with the comment, "Look it up yourself, Newton." Whether the epithet reflected a conscious decision on his part to introduce me to the Laws of Motion (and their application to the art of canoeing), or whether he was dreaming of watching apples fall on a sunny day and blurted out the name unreflectively, I'll never know.

Some days later, after I had mastered the names and purposes of the various strokes, I signed up again for sixth period canoeing, this time voluntarily. Educational theory in the late 1950s had it that the discovery method was the best way to learn a new skill. So I wound up in a sixteen foot canoe alone, paddling right. There was a brisk breeze on the lake and it wasn't long before I had done two or three donuts on my un-planned voyage to the far end of Prep Bay. Each time I got the canoe pointed directly upwind and took a forward stroke, the bow went sharply left. Faithful to Perry's gospel, I immediately would do a reverse sweep. Yet, far from realigning the canoe, the sweep merely moved me backwards at the same declination. So the pattern established itself: one bow stroke, three reverse sweeps, a complete donut, thirty feet farther down wind; one bow stroke, three reverse sweeps, a complete donut, thirty feet still farther down wind. I knew Perry admonished that, to move the bow to the side on which you are paddling, use a reverse sweep. I also knew that it wasn't working.

Towards the end of the period one of the canoe instructors paddled down to rescue me. Until then it had been common practice for lost souls to grab onto the instructor's painter to be ceremonially towed back to the canoe dock. But after I had ex-plained how I got to where I was, and after I carefully rehearsed the theory according to Perry my rescuer declined to take me in tow. Setting off to assist others, and ever-faithful to his beloved discovery method, he simply said, "Once you get off-line, use a front sweep to spin the canoe quickly in the direction it's going; when you're about three-quarters of the way around, start to do the bow stroke again." Slowly, I crabbed back up the bay in a new pattern: one bow stroke, two front sweeps, three-quarters of a donut, five bow strokes, thirty feet upwind; one bow stroke, two front sweeps, three-quarters of a donut, five bow strokes, thirty more feet upwind. About half an hour later, when I finally regained the canoe dock, he enquired of me how it went. I carefully explained that his front sweep technique was successful, but wrong. Perry's book mandated a reverse sweep for such cases. To which he casually replied, "Oh, didn't I tell you ... we call that the windy weather reverse sweep."

There is a striking parallel in this anecdote with a perva-sive problem in late 20th century legal practice. Too often our response as jurists to intractable socioeconomic puzzles is to ig-nore the counsel of experience and stick unflinchingly to the counsel of textbook wisdom. Several unfortunate consequences flow from this atavistic reflex. First, jurists display an unwarranted faith that written law, and especially constitutional documents such as charters of rights, can actually solve problems of freedom, equality and procedural fairness; second, they have a naive commitment to the categories of knowledge and experience set out by law (and the constitution) as the only way of apprehending and understanding the world around them. Let me illustrate how these themes converge by considering aspects of section 7 of the 1982 Canadian Charter of Rights and Freedoms, which provides:

Everyone has the right to life, liberty and security of the person and the right not to be deprived thereof except in accordance with the principles of fundamental justice.[2]

I grant that this brief statement of virtue has the ring of authenticity. But would the average evicted tenant, welfare recipient, resident of a mental institution, or victim of a traffic fatality consequent upon a high-speed police chase really believe that the condition of civil liberties in Canada dramatically changed for the better on April 15, 1982? Clearly, no provision like section 7 was needed to curb the excesses of Premiers Hepburn, Aberhart or Duplessis. But equally clearly, section 7 would not have prevented the imposition of conscription by fraudulent electoral practices in 1917, the dislocation of Japanese-Canadians during World War II, or the invocation of the War Measures Act in 1970. Nor would section 7 provide a shield from the enormous social costs imposed by big business and big labour.

The point I am developing has a further, non-Canadian dimension. To my knowledge, no state possessed of a constitutional guarantee similar to section 7 had a demonstrably better civil libertarian record than Canada. Certainly, the French treatment of immigrants, of Algerians and of Basque terrorists, and the history of US legislation in respect of indians, blacks, asians, anarchists and communists disqualifies these two oft-cited paragons from claiming moral superiority on this score. On the available evidence, without a concerted effort by citizens to be vigilant about freedom and equality, a constitutional prescription of due process is no more meaningful (or effective) than Perry's prescription of the reverse sweep.

This brings me to the second theme. Legislative provisions such as section 7 can actually be stultifying, because a constitutional text tends to monopolize discourse about socioeconomic policy choices. This can be seen by comparing section 7 with the analogous provision of the US Constitution. That Constitution's Fifth Amendment provides, in part:

No person shall ... be deprived of life, liberty, or property, without due process of law;

Apart from the substitution of the term "principles of fundamental justice" for the term "due process of law", the notable difference between section 7 and the Fifth Amendment is that "security of the person" is protected in the former, while "property" is protected in the latter. This difference is less significant than one might think.

Notwithstanding the absence of the phrase "property" and the evident intention of the proponents of section 7 to exclude it, many jurists today are preoccupied with its resurrection as a judicially protected constitutional right. Creative interpretations of other phrases, in particular the right to "security of the person," have most often been the vehicle of this resurrection. Paradoxically, in the United States, many forms of government social assistance program (which, if anything, are directed to the economic security of the person) are characterized as property for the same purpose: to ground judicial review of government decisions leading to their deprivation. To dissimulate the protection of property as the guarantee of economic "security of the person" is to surrender common sense to the tyranny of a constitutional formula, and is no less disingenuous than to characterize a "front sweep" as a "windy weather reverse sweep."

If such fictions are, indeed, the pathology of the legal system, if they arise when established rules do not neatly fit the social life they presumably regulate, the reasonable reader might well wonder why they are not simply abolished by legislation? That is, if security of the person is not intended to cover property rights, why doesn't Parliament simply define security of the person so as to exclude property rights? The answer parallels that already suggested in relation to the immediate impact of the Charter. The legislative abolition of a fiction is unlikely to affect the patterns of human interaction which initially gave rise to it. Legislation may well change the rhetoric by which property rights are advanced; it has a limited capacity to counter the urge to acquire and to own, or to suppress human innovation in justifying fictitious characterizations of property. To change Perry's prescription from "reverse sweep" to "front sweep" in windy weather neither calms the storm nor prevents for very long the emergence of fictional "windy weather front sweeps" such as the now familiar C-stroke.

The canoe, like all human artifacts, is not just an ornament. It can be used to accomplish a variety of human purposes. In central Canadian post-war folklore, surely the most romanticized of these purposes is the canoe trip. To this mythology I turn for my second example. Let us assume that a scheme of radical or direct democracy is no way to run a canoe trip. However the initial responsibilities like choice of route, camp site management and so on are defined, and however democratic the pre-trip processes by which these responsibilities are allocated among trip members, once the trip is on the water a quasi-hierarchical management regime must prevail. Let me be clear about my use of the terms hierarchical and horizontal. The distinction between them does not lie in the fact of dictatorial powers being conceded to the hierarchical leader. Even in the army, more than brute force is needed to maintain effective authority. Usually some shared commitment, to defeating the enemy or, in the case of a canoe trip, to an enjoyable trip, is the backdrop against which all authority is exercised. Moreover, a degree of responsiveness to the needs and wishes of those being led is necessary to nurture continuing confidence in trip leaders. By the third or fourth day, no leader can command just by ordering. Within the limits of these two minimal constraints, we might say that members of the expedition either explicitly or tacitly confer upon trip leaders, each in their own domain, a wide margin of discretion to take major decisions.

Yet a canoe trip is not a momentary event, and the interpersonal dynamic of participants is constantly shifting. In the routine of trip decision-making, that is, in the pattern of minor exercises of responsibility, the increments of discretion will vary among trip leaders. While guide and cook may at the outset have commanded equal authority, the exigencies of weather, route, personality and pure hazard operate to modify that authority. Not only may the structure of authority as between designated leader and trip members change, but also in those cases where different responsibilities like route, navigation, campsite, or kitchen have been allocated, the boundaries between these (no matter how clearly defined at the outset) are constantly shifting. Should the campsite manager prove ineffectual, the guide may well end up making the real decisions about choice of camp site (ostensibly determined, of course, by the exigencies of tomorrow's paddling schedule), and the cook may effectively take control over camp site layout, including placement of tents and allocation of on-site tasks (ostensibly determined, of course, by the complexity of the meal to be cooked, or the need to finish dinner prior to an impending storm, or whatever). If left to its own devices, ineffectual leadership can breed anarchy, as when for example, tents are located haphazardly, no common toilet site is chosen and dug, and campsite layout is decided by the most aggressive.

The reason why collateral authority tends to expand in the face of weak leadership is not hard to divine. Disorganization in one sector has a spill-over effect. If tent site choice is to the swiftest, inappropriate tactical manoeuvering on the water (including in rapids) to gain an advantage may result. The guide's judgement then becomes open to evaluation not only as to its quality for purposes of safety on the water, but also as to its potential impact on camp site management. Moreover, the authority exercised by other trip leaders loses a part of its moral foundation by ricochet. A loss of confidence in one leader rarely translates directly into increased confidence in the others. Rather a positive and subtle shift of initiative and jurisdiction is necessary to maintain overall authority. It follows that whatever the original allocation of decision-making authority, and whatever the leadership dynamic at the outset of a trip, tacit accommodations resulting from the ongoing interaction of trip members shapes and defines how the allocated authority is actually exercised.

This commonplace experience of most canoe-trippers is, regrettably, lost on many contemporary constitutional law theorists. Apart from its formality, a constitution is, after all, not unlike the pre-trip organization meeting. It is a constitutive process which allocates authority between levels of government, among branches of government, and between citizen and state.

Like the authority of any given trip leader, the authority of a constitution is never fixed. It may be changed in two main ways: by formal amendment, as we have recently witnessed with the 1982 *Constitution Act;* and by tacit accommodation among the principal actors on the political stage. As a legal phenomenon, the first (that is, the process of making law) has attracted most attention. But the second, the development and evolution of constitutional conventions, is that which best reflects how political authority is actually exercised. The Patriation References[3] of 1982 and 1984 and the current Meech Lake Accord illustrate effectively the place of implicit law in our constitutional arrangements.

In 1981, after several years of negotiation relating to the patriation of the British North America Act, 1867, the federal government drafted a "Proposed Resolution for a Joint Address to Her Majesty the Queen respecting the Constitution of Canada" under which the constitution would be amended at the behest of the Canadian Parliament and over the opposition of several provincial governments. Three provinces, Manitoba, Quebec and Newfoundland, brought legal proceedings, whose ultimate effect was to compel the Supreme Court of Canada to decide whether the law required a substantial measure of provincial consent to any constitutional amendments affecting their legislative authority. By a seven to two majority, the Court held that as a matter of law (that is, as a matter of the interpretation of the original allocation of decision-making authority in the 1867 BNA Act) no such provincial consent was required. Yet four of the seven ju ges comprising the majority also held that as a matter of convention (that is, as a matter of constitutional propriety given how the powers initially allocated had actually been exercised over the past century) the consent of a substantial number of provinces to such amendments was required.

To arrive at this conclusion, these four justices carefully examined the practice of Canadian federalism since 1867. They concluded both that there never had been an amendment affecting provincial rights without their consent, and that the federal government had always acted as if some degree of provincial consent to such amendments were required. The actual practice of constitutional amendment, coupled with a belief in the appropriateness of the practice, amounts to a judicially cognizable phenomenon. Tacit accommodation to the realities of a federal system alters the initial allocation of decision-making authority, just as tacit accommodation to the exigencies of trip leadership alters the discretion of leaders.

The true nature of these accommodations can be seen in the continuing saga of constitutional amendment leading right up to the Meech Lake Accord. Following agreement by all other provinces to a series of constitutional amendments negotiated after this first Patriation Reference, the government of Quebec sought to have the Supreme Court of Canada declare either that unanimous provincial consent to constitutional amendments was required, or that Quebec had a veto over proposed amendments to the BNA Act. In a unanimous judgement, the Supreme Court affirmed that neither result followed as a matter of law and that there also was no constitutional convention to either effect. This second Patriation Reference confirmed the Constitution Act, 1982 as a matter of law and convention. So the situation stood until the Meech Lake Accord proceeded to recognize the constitutional equivalent of the grievance of an incompetent campsite manager.

There are those, of course, who see Meech Lake as a positive step towards "bringing Quebec into the Constitution." But this ignores the lesson of the Charter. The absence of the Meech Lake Accord will not keep a willing Quebec on the margins of the Canadian state; nor will a Meech Lake Accord *ipso facto* incorporate a reluctant Quebec into the Canadian community. But by failing to recognize the subtle interplay of made law and implicit law the Meech Lake negotiations have prematurely crystallized alternative allocations of authority before the actual exercise of power under previous constitutional allocations has been evaluated. Do we want to emulate the banana republics which proclaim a new constitution each time a government changes? Nation states, like canoe trips, can accommodate only a limited number of late-night pow wows at which the competent and the incompetent, the thoughtful and the impulsive, the satisfied and the malcontent, engage in group therapy. By acknowledging in the Patriation References the place of conventions as judicially cognizable statements of constitutional propriety, the Supreme Court officially sanctioned the canoe-tripper's wisdom; unhappily, Meech Lake now appears to have abandoned the insight.

How does this discussion bear on the canoe in Canadian culture? Two American themes have dominated Canadian law since the end of the Second World War. The first of these is a preoccupation with libertarian responses to social legislation: here the underlying ethic is simply that "government is bad." The other theme is galloping legalism. Here, the underlying ethic is that "lawyers are the best defenders of freedom." In my view, neither of these preoccupations deserves much currency in Canada.

A more heterodox political and legal culture holds sway north of the 49th parallel, in that there is no hegemonic view of what it means to be Canadian. The expression "un-Canadian" rings false. In fact, it is even hard to think what would be the predicate to the phrase "as Canadian as ..." The absence of a vision of the paradigm makes explicit legal definition such as that found in the US Constitution impossible. Second, no proselytizing zeal about the virtues of confrontation characterizes Canadian legal values. If the lawsuit serves as the 20th century cowboy shoot-out in the US, the federal-provincial conference is Canada's 20th century Family Compact or Chateau Clique. The absence of adversarialness makes deference to authority a legitimate feature of Canadian legal life.

Just as the canoe and its myths have characterized our past as a people, the lessons to be drawn from these tales ought to characterize our future.

Notes

1 Perry, Ronald H. *The Canoe and You*. Toronto: Dent, 1948.

2 Constitution Act, 1982, Part I, ss 1-34, Canada Act, 1982, Ch 11, sched B (U.K.)

3 Re Resolution to Amend the Constitution, [1981] 1, S.C.R. 753: Re Quebec Veto [1982] 2, S.C.R. 793.

Probing Canoe Trips
for Persistent Meaning

James Raffan

What of this fabulous country
Now that we have it reduced to a few hot hours
And sun-burn on our backs?[1]

Visions of canoe tripping filter into my imagination long after
the paddling is done. The dreams are fleeting; it is as if there
is a theatrical scrim separating paddling from daily life. When
the light is right, when circumstances trigger a
recollection—maybe a white bird against the sun—I see through
the barrier and into the mythical substance of the canoeing
experience: a twitch of the eye and the journey of the imagination vanishes from view. But something lingers—a feeling, a
sense of confidence, an abiding peace—something from the
canoeing experience or from the wilderness itself.

My premise is that canoeing plays a significant role in
people's lives beyond the simple act of paddling. By extension,
I hope to show that the canoe's significance for individuals can
also shape public life and hence, come to bear on Canadian culture. As such, this essay is not so much focussed on the canoe,
the vehicle, as on the canoe *experience* and its influence on
Canadian life.

Wilderness Travel is not limited to the mountains (or to the rivers
and lakes); its lessons permeate our whole lives, and we are subtly
changed by it. One eventually becomes a Wilderness Traveller in
daily life.[2]

To be a wilderness traveller in daily life means having a
value system shaped and informed by trail life. "Wilderness

travellers in daily life" share this value system, and a special kind of belonging derived from elemental encounters with the land. Picking up on that notion, my probe for persistent meaning in canoe trips has three three thought lines: *recollection* of three storm-stayed days in a wet tent; *understanding* about the world that exists apart from canoeing; *construction* of mechanisms by which the essence of the canoeing experience is transmuted to the more complex matters of daily life.

Robertson Davies has written that "The Canadian is, in intellectual matters, a slob."[3] Good works in the Canadian experience, says Davies, are cheap in comparison with solitary psychological hard work. It may be that Davies has looked in all the wrong places because there is no better spot for "solitary psychological hard work" than inside a tent on the tundra during a violent, 72-hour, arctic storm. Three such days provide moments of intense fear and concentration on one end of the scale, and hours of back-aching boredom on the other, with a great variety of imagined journeys in between. Come to the shores of the Elk River for an example which shows the potential of the canoeing experience for enriching daily life.

Date	July 23
Time	8:30 p.m.
Temperature	4° Celsius
Wind	Near Gale Force (SE)
Latitude	61° North
Nearest City	Lynn Lake, Man., 300 miles SE
Precipitation	Rain with ice pellets

Four of us had been forced from the river by a front that closed the sky like an eyelid. In our frantic effort to get tents secured before the storm, an arctic tern hovered effortlessly on the gale. While laying out the tent, a muffled screech from behind delivered a flurried splat on my hood. Picking up the tent, we ran for the lone spruce on the site. From there it was plain to see that the bird was nesting right on the ground not ten metres from our chosen spot. Better not camp there.

The tern was in the midst of incubating four neatly camouflaged eggs in a fist-sized scraping in the gravel, devoid of grass, fur, or feather. There was nothing "nestly" about it. The bird's aggressive behaviour and spartan nest were definitely not more interesting than the challenge of finding a tent site before the storm. If anything, I resented the bird for getting in the way — to say nothing of the way it had soiled my kelly green, state-of-the-art cagoule. It never occurred to me at the time how simply and elegantly the tern and its impending family rose to the occasion of this storm.

It took a complicated assemblage of fibreglass, nylon, aluminum and stray rocks heaped on wire tent pegs for us to build a shelter. Our nest was an expensive geodesic dome, now grotesquely skewed by the wind and anchored to large chunks of the Canadian Shield with taut guy ropes humming in chorus. Even then, as we would soon learn, this combination of neolithic and petrochemical technologies would come a distant second to the tern's solution to the shelter problem.

Two of us squeezed down in our fibre-filled bags, placed packs on the windward side of the tent, and tried to sleep. It was one of the most exciting moments of my life to be there, on the tundra, in touch with my vulnerability, and revelling in the elemental simplicity of the situation. We were in contact with the land, with nature and all its forces. This would not be a storm we would hear about on the news. This would not be a agent whose effects would be beyond our personal experience. Our solution to the storm problem was not nearly as elegant or as well developed as the tern's but, like the tern, we were on the brink of an opportunity to test our capabilities and resources. There were no peripheral issues as I lay in the tent that night. The objective was simple: to get through the storm without dying.

The opportunity to focus on a serious problem without extraneous complications is an unsung virtue of wilderness travel. According to psychologists, people have difficulty concentrating in daily life because their voluntary attention mechanisms get pushed beyond effective limits:

In wilderness what is interesting to perceive tends to be what one needs to know in order to act. For many people the purposes one carries into the wilderness also fit closely with the demands that the wilderness makes: what one intends to do is also what one must do in order to survive.[4]

There is freedom of mind and spirit that creeps into one's consciousness with the realization that everything that can be done to secure the tent has been done, and that, providing those measures hold (and they're as secure as the practice you've had with other storms), while the world is reduced by the storm to this simple set of cause and effect relationships, the only thing left to do is sleep. And sleep we did — the comatose sleep of an exhausted body and an untroubled mind.

I awoke at two a.m. in the northern twilight to find that the tent had been recurved by the wind, leaving the soaked nylon wall pressed to my sleeping bag. It took a moment to fathom that the tent was unravelling in the wind. Under the stress of gale force winds the poles had taken on a curious, skewed bell curve shape. Reaching to sit up into the lumen of the tent that remained, my hand splashed in a deep puddle.

Awakened and apprised of the details of the situation my partner and I sat quietly in enveloping fear and calmly discussed the possibility of the two of us, in the tent, rolling willy nilly across the tundra and into the river. The beauty and the immediacy of this predicament went unappreciated at the time. What we had going for us was an unparalleled opportunity for improvisation and resourcefulness.

Simply put, we were in fear for our lives. Our shelter was in danger of destruction. The weather (based on a quick look out the door) appeared unlikely to change in the foreseeable future. The outside temperature was near freezing; clearly, without our tent it would be impossible to stay dry enough or warm enough to survive. There was a possibility of running to the domicile of our companions, but they were very likely busy with similar problems. There was no home to run to, no building to cower in and nothing except that which we had with us to maintain life.

The prospect of rolling into the river seemed too real to leave doing nothing as an attractive option. Two possibilities remained. We could attempt to bunk in with the other crew. This, unfortunately, would leave our tent unanchored, and increase the possibility of losing it altogether. Putting four people in a tent that sleeps only two would also cause overcrowding, though on the up side, this was probably something we could all cope with for a short period of time, and there was value in being together in the face of adversity. But ... losing a tent (or two) would be catastrophic. The only remaining option was to protect the tent from the wind.

Suspending the story momentarily, it is worth noting the value of experiencing helplessness before nature. As in many wilderness situations, our group was confronted with circumstances over which we had absolutely no control. Regardless of individual skills, knowledge, or competencies, everyone was equally powerless. Regardless of previous shared experiences, the elemental fact that everyone is equally incapable of changing the weather was a potent force binding the group together. The experience engendered new perspectives and new possibilities. Momentarily, or for as long as the storm might last, each member of the group had the opportunity to explore the other group members' characteristics and reactions in new and productive ways.

The results of universal powerlessness can be seen in our response to the wind threat. What might have been a competitive event, two crews struggling simultaneously with the same problem, actually turned into a mutually supportive search for a workable solution. Knowing there was nothing that could be done about the wind, one pair opted to reinforce its tent from within by sitting inside with backs against the windward wall, arms holding the poles that were most likely to break under the stress. Unfortunately, this method was predicated on the occupants being awake for the duration of the storm. While they were doing that, my partner was outside working on another idea.

With me inside the tent for ballast, my partner went out in search of an obstacle to break the wind. The lone tree looked more wind-blown than our tent, and there was no guarantee that we would be able to move the tent in that direction without it blowing away. The canoes were tied to rocks and bushes near the shore; clearly, if one of them caught the wind, it would catapult end over end across the tundra. The only immediately movable item big enough and heavy enough to withstand the wind was our large wooden wanigan filled with staple foods, pots and spices. Fortunately, the box, when dragged to the windward side of the tent, diverted sufficient wind to allow the fatigued tent poles to rise and again form an approximation of a dome. Heavy food packs did the same for the other tent. Back we went to bed, feeling satisfied that the threat had been eased, at least for the moment.

The following morning, the wanigan solution seemed to be holding, but after twelve hours confinement my back was sore, and we were decidedly peckish. It was low growling hunger that finally drove two expeditionaries back out into the storm at about three p.m.   We collected a small gas stove, a pot, cheese, crackers, and gorp from our soaked food packs and scampered back to our respective tents. Having been exposed for a minute or two, I was wet from hood to boot. The last thing my partner wanted was more water inside, so I passed in the food and stove, removed my garments quickly, turned them inside out, and rolled into the tent. It seemed an awful fuss to get a bite to eat, no casual tug on the refrigerator door, like home.

Concentration on hunger and its resolution is for many wilderness travellers a refreshing return to what Abraham Maslow called the basis of personality.   For Maslow, the development of personality is a life-long progression through a hierarchy of needs. To come to a realization of self, or as Maslow put it, to become "self-actualized," one must satisfy a series of needs: physiological, safety, belongingness, esteem, and needs for growth.[5] One of the strengths and deeply seated joys of working to satisfy hunger is to become reacquainted with physiological needs at the base of Maslow's hierarchy. In daily life, in a world that often takes for granted the primal needs such as sustenance and security, it may well be that barriers to self-realization are nothing more than a lapse in recognition of more fundamental needs that constitute the base of Maslow's pyramid.

The simple act of preparing a pot of hot tea and a plate of cheese and crackers to be delivered to tent-bound companions is in itself the realization of a physiological need. This act also builds for the preparer a sense of belonging in the group, and maybe even esteem from those who were served. It is my experience, having made this effort on the shores of the Elk River, that there really is a strong basis of good feeling and confidence that comes from sharing a meal under trying circumstances. In an age when growth and self-actualization are attractive goals, wilderness experience reminds us all that such lofty needs are predicated on a stack of simpler ones that are often neglected because they are so easily obtained.

Safe travel also involves familiarity with a wide range of necessary skills such as knotting, fire lighting, map reading. There is something intensely satisfying about lying in a damp sleeping bag, sipping hot tea, knowing that it is only simple skills of hand and mind which create such comfort. In such a primitive environment, where rhythms of sleep and waking take a natural course, where mere sustenance requires effort, where elimination is an adventure, it is the connection with all aspects of one's life and capabilities that builds within the soul an enduring sense of satisfaction and possibility. Using Maslow's construct, Alan R. Drengson described the phenomenon this way: "Wilderness travel addresses not only the intellect, but makes demands on the resources of the whole person. It requires the capacity to respond intelligently with all of one's emotional, physical, intellectual, and spiritual energies."[6]

Back in the storm, a seam gave way to the badgering wind. With tape and stitches we did our best to make it right, and the patch seemed to hold. What might have been panic born of eroding shelter, the challenge of fixing the tent came as a welcome break in our monotonous existence. Still turned away from the storm, we played backgammon with little magnetic counters on a tiny folding board that would never lie flat on the mess. By game five there was no comfortable way to lean, sit or otherwise settle myself to see the board. Enough of that. The weather continued to howl without. I lay back with a book about three men who lived and died in the area through which we were about to travel.

The Legend of John Hornby[7] is a gripping tale of a cavalier Englishman who entered the Thelon River valley in the summer of 1927 with his nephew and another man, expecting to live for the winter on the flesh of fat caribou. They missed the migration and the three died a tortured death of starvation. They lived in a tiny cabin built into a hillside, not unlike this tiny confine in which I lay. I looked at the bug stains, the water marks, the socks and gloves drying on an overhead line. I listened to the wind whack the side of the tent. I watched water drip from beleaguered seams, and suddenly felt attached to history—Hornby's history—and strangely afraid. It was a curious attraction and repulsion reminiscent of Margaret Atwood's comment: "Every culture has its exemplary dead people, its hagiography of landscape martyrs, those unfortunates who, by their bad ends, seem to sum up in one grisly episode what may be lurking behind the next rock for all of us, all of us who enter the territory they once claimed as theirs."[8]

By then the cheese, crackers, gorp, and tea had been digested. I had to void. Dressing once again, I left the tent, and saw the tern. The bird sat contentedly on the nest, by now inured to us. Amazing, I thought, that this bundle of feathers and nest-building skill could weather the storm with such ease.

Returning to the tent, with the tern's matter-of-fact existence very much in mind, I looked around at the trappings on the tent floor. We weren't terns, but ours was a simple life nonetheless: a sleeping bag for warmth, food for sustenance, partners for support and companionship; the tent for shelter, a game for entertainment, a book for pleasure; and outside: a pack for storage, a canoe for transportation. For all the problems of being windbound—getting off schedule, keeping occupied, staying fit, keeping fed, maintaining warmth—this was an uncomplicated life we were leading. It was the wilderness equivalent of the double-edged freedom celebrated in the hobo's anthem "King of the Road." Indeed we were living a life of simplicity set out by circumstances: "No phone, no pool, no pets." It was heavenly!

Just then, the buzz of a Twin Otter aircraft came our way on the wind. As the plane passed directly overhead, a new kind of fear scurried out from a dark corner of the subconscious world, a kind of fear that we hadn't felt since beginning the trip, a fear associated with people. The flypast, and the fear, was enough to rally all the troops to full storm dress.

We watched the plane circle and drop behind a hill for landing. Thoughts raged of family deaths, police searches, something catastrophic enough to deliver a message to a relative pinned down on the tundra. We worried past the nest—the tern rose to greet us but quickly returned to its mewing nestlings—and to the top of a small rise behind the camp. The view of a pilot refueling the plane from drums cached on a distant beach let us know that the adrenaline spurt was in vain—the pilot had no idea we were there.

The event amplified the difference between the predictably unpredictable (but nevertheless brutal) challenges engineered by the quirks of nature and the unpredictably unpredictable turns of human imagination and catastrophe. And within this realization was the appreciation of having communication with the rest of the world cut off. It made me ponder how much time I spend wondering and worrying about media information over which I have no control. It made me know that sometimes it is better not to know, better to attend solely to those concerns over which one has influence. It made me appreciate the genuine comfort and support in our little group.

When all of the falderal associated with the plane had passed, it was only then that we realized that if a plane was flying, the weather must be improving. The plane was from Yellowknife, to the west, and we reasoned that, if it had flown from its base, then the weather coming our way must be better. Without delay—after nearly three days layover—we struck camp and headed down river. It was a jubilant, but bed sore, return to the river.

This storm, and all our ruminations, symbolizes the potential of wilderness for meaningful human experience and powerful learning. I'm convinced that long time travellers of the wild bear the richness of the wilderness experience in their daily demeanour. It's inescapable. But it's also largely taken as a matter of course. Most often people talk in rather figurative terms about the power of wilderness. John Muir, wilderness philosopher and great believer said, "(in wilderness) cares drop off like autumn leaves."[9] Thoreau and others said the same, in other ways:

We need the tonic of wilderness, to wade sometimes in marshes where
the bittern and meadowhen lurk and hear the booming of the snipe;
to smell the whispering sedge where only some wilder and more solitary fowl builds her nest, and the mink crawls with with its belly
close to the ground.[10]

That is why when after a day of battle, your tent is pitched at last
in the lee of some sheltering cliff, the canoe up safe and dry, and
supper on the way, there is an exaltation that only canoemen
know.[11]

You would go to nature for your metaphysical fix—your reassurance
that the world makes sense. It's a reassurance that there's something
behind it all and it's good, you come back to where men are, to where
men are messing things up, because men tend to, and you come back
with a new ability to relate to your fellow man and to help your fellow
man relate to each other.[12]

What sets a canoeing expedition apart is that it purifies you more
rapidly and inescapably than any other. Travel 1000 miles by train
and you are a brute; pedal 500 miles on a bicycle and you remain
basically a bourgeois; paddle 100 miles in a canoe and you are already a child of nature.[13]

I should like very much to live here forever. It's sorcery. It's not our
world at all; it's like another star.[14]

There is literal transfer of superficial values from
wilderness experience to daily life. However, the message in the
writing of people who have been deeply moved by wilderness
experiences is that there are attachments between the experience itself and daily life which are much more subtle and profound. But with effort, close observation, and sensitivity, distinct
patterns of transfer begin to emerge. These patterns form what
might be called the myth of the canoeing experience, the subconscious or ingrained understandings about the enterprise
which shape the way we think. Myth, in this context, was explained by writer David Cayley this way: "myth reaches beyond
... the continuous psychosis of human history to reach a higher
dimension of time. It belongs to the eternal present of the
psyche, that timelessness of the unconscious on which Jung
commented. As such, myth is present in all societies ..."[15] It

may be that metaphor is the mechanism through which the myth of a canoeing experience is born.

Several writers have pondered the metaphorical basis of meaning transferred from wilderness to daily life. Like Cayley, Stephen Bacon[16] invoked the teaching of psychiatrist C.G. Jung and presented ten archetypes or patterns in the transfer of meaning from wilderness experience to daily life. The argument is that archetypes (original patterns), of which there are many, are reproduced in the psyche of every person, and further, that these mental structures define and delineate the manner in which the world is perceived.

Archetype is an intriguing idea for making sense of the wilderness experience. When Bacon talks about rite of passage, sacred space, justice, fate, mother, family, leader, hermit, hero, and ascent to heaven archetypes, there is a ring of authenticity in them, especially when considered in light of three days spent in a storm-bound tent. Bacon's analysis, however, is limited to archetypes as they relate to the idiosyncratic features of Outward Bound wilderness courses. Taking the strength of Jung's archetype notion as pioneered in the wilderness context by Bacon, and applying it to themes from Canadian literature, and to understandings from my own experience, new patterns emerge to describe the mechanism by which wilderness essence is transferred to daily life.

Marked by the Wild,[17] an anthology of literature shaped by the Canadian wilderness, is richly resonant with the existence of archetypes in the psyche of the everyday paddler. Say Bruce Litteljohn and John Pearce in the book's introduction: "There is a considerable body of Canadian writing in which wilderness and the natural world operate in a subtle and indirect way—as image and metaphor rather than content or context." To support their contention, they quote author George Woodcock who said, "Many of our writers do not use the primitive landscape directly, yet somewhere in their visions and their forms the wilderness will always lurk."

The first chapter in *Marked by the Wild* is entitled "An Elemental Song: The Non-Human World." It advances the idea that the wilderness is omnipotent—it was, can, is, and will be capable of self-regulation and majesty without human help or intervention. In me, and in people I've met on the trail, there is a strong wilderness lesson that places the land first, with people as but one more species in the overall scheme of things. This pattern might be called the "ecologue" archetype. Its significance is the way in which it helps people come to a biocentric view of the world, to find a sense of kinship and belonging in nature. I suppose strong support for the existence of this archetype is the number of environmental activists who have had some sort of meaningful wilderness journey. It is as if the wilderness must first speak personally to those who will ultimately come to be advocates for its preservation.

Bacon does not include anything that resembles the ecologue, although in the community archetype he hints at Outward Bound participants as members of some larger natural or world community. I think that the ecologue pattern is likely to promote awareness of other enduring metaphorical patterns in nature, such as the river—with its rough water, smooth water, riparian community, impassable falls, and ever-moving flow—as an icon for life itself. The value of ecologue is the abiding sense of belonging to the biosphere which it confers on those who meet it.

Bacon does describe the sacred space archetype that characterizes wilderness as a numinous place that always leaves its magical and unexpected mark on visitors:

The power of this archetype is such that human beings are unconsciously prepared to recognize a concrete manifestation of the pattern when they encounter it in the world. ... Sacred Space means that the (person) has implicitly accepted the possibility—or even the probability—that some kind of powerful transformation may occur.[18]

This pattern looms large in *Marked by the Wild,* and in my own experience. Litteljohn and Pearce talk about "Crooked Nerves Made Straight: The Benign Wilderness" and a collection of writings they call "Never Quite the Same: Wilderness as Self-Discovery." Both chapters develop the idea of sacred space from which protagonists return home changed by the wilderness.

When wilderness removes the ills of the civilized world, one can find in the sacred space archetype a sin and redemption metaphor. This interpretation is supported by Willi Unsoeld's statement, previously quoted, about nature reassuring us that something behind the world is good. Thoreau wrote about the "tonic of wilderness."[19] In an essay about Thoreau, Robert Louis Stephenson on the strength of such statements, called Thoreau a "skulker" and a "mere escapist."[20] Interestingly, Stephenson later retracted this opinion, perhaps as a reflection of the truth in the sacred space archetype.

Another significant archetype for canoe travellers is the hero or heroic quest. The most complete consideration of this archetype is William Closson James' article, "The Quest Pattern and the Canoe Trip." James describes the parallels and issues a caution:

All of the ingredients (are) there: the departure from the known, the voyage into the unknown, and the return to civilization; the obstacles of high winds, rough waters, brutal portages, dissension, and long dreary days; the unexpected pleasures of new vistas, of wildlife seen, of achievements and minor triumphs, and the joy of one's companions; the sense of participation in a primitive reality, or the re-enactment of an archetypal event, the sloughing off of the inessential and the experience of renewal.

An encounter with that wilderness by means of a canoe trip is a repetition of the quest pattern as described in its most familiar form by Joseph Campbell. But I want also to suggest that this particular version of the quest has its perils too, so that it can be misapplied or misunderstood with results that are often unfortunate and sometimes disastrous.[21]

It may be that this archetype is exclusively male in its orientation. The idea of heroic conquest seems foreign to female sensibilities. Nevertheless, to greater or lesser extents, canoeists do use this construct to transfer trials and tribulations from the trail to troubles at work. It is also worth considering the extent to which this archetype lives in the mind of non-paddlers and armchair adventurers, who tend to perceive wilderness veterans as heroes of a kind, thereby reinforcing heroic imagery in a venturer's psyche. Thinking back to those three days in the Elk Lake tent, amid such recollections in the dim recesses of my imagination are strong parallels to Jason and his tribulations en route to the coveted golden fleece.

At the same time, wilderness experience can reinforce destructive behaviours and attitudes that do not promote wellness and growth whether away or at home. This might be called the "Rambo" variation on the hero archetype. Consider those who enter the wilderness for short periods of time, and only with mechanized support such as four-wheel-drive vehicles or outboard motors. The introduced excess of power reinforces destructive notions arising from the Judeo-Christian axiom of human "dominion" over the earth and all its creatures. The Rambo pattern shares the anthropocentric viewpoint of people Litteljohn and Pearce described as "too accustomed to thinking in terms of natural resources—trees as pulp and paper, seals as fur coats, waterfalls as hydro-electric power—to recognize the integrity and autonomy of wilderness."22

Although my wilderness sensibilities are offended by such an archetype, I need only remember winter visits with a trapper friend to unoccupied moose hunting cabins on Quebec's Dumoine River—replete with spent shells, beer bottles, and wall spreads of pinups—to know that Rambo lives. There is a frightening archetype in the woods and on the streets that embodies the only moments of true power and control these men have in their lives. What I fear is that this pattern tacitly reinforces negative attitudes in everyone who travels in the wilderness, myself included. It is troubling and humbling to realize that all of us use energy overkill in our approach to the wild. There is a little of Rambo in everyone.

There is an archetypal pattern which is somewhat antithetical to the heroic quest (and more feminine in its bearing) and which could be called the "partner." Relational phenomena of sensitivity, tolerance, support and understanding emerge during canoe trips. The one who ventures into the storm to fetch food and the one who stays dry and receives it are bonded in a special way, like the terns perhaps. This archetype turns the cultural microcosm of canoe pairings in limited and isolated circumstances into a powerful reflective tool capable of colouring interpersonal relationships at home. The partner archetype gives river friendships special significance in the cacophony and superficiality of daily life. And of equal importance is the discovered ability to forge similar bonds of partnership at home.

There are other archetypal patterns which can emerge from encounters with wilderness and which can help explain the persistent power of the canoe trip experience. There is the explorer—a version of the quest pattern; justice—reinforcing fair consequence of individual action; leader—pattern of influence and decision making; native—the link to aboriginal and birthplace roots; and "Canadian"—the realization of a historical enterprise and ancestral heritage common to every citizen of this country. No doubt there are more.

I have outlined the case for the contention that the canoe experience, through transfer to everyday life, plays a role—maybe an important, if unsung one—in Canadian culture. There is more than suffering to canoe tripping, a lot more than we at first thought. Wouldn't it be exciting if we could learn to understand the operational archetypes in a way that would allow us to purposefully use the wilderness to heal societal ills? Wouldn't it be satisfying if we intellectual slobs, as Robertson Davies called us, found ways to make the benefits of wilderness experiences grow long after we're back home? Barry Lopez writes, "It is easy to underestimate the power of a long-term association with the land, not just with a specific spot but with the span of it in memory and imagination, how it fills, for example, one's dreams."[23] The storm, the tent, the tern have demonstrated their power to stimulate meaning and to shape culture.

Notes

1 Le Pan, D. in Litteljohn, B. and Pearce, J. *Marked by the Wild.* Toronto: McClelland and Stewart, 1973, pp 126-7.

2 Drengson, A. "Wilderness Travel as an Art and as a Paradigm for Outdoor Education," *Quest* 3(1) 1980, pp 110- 120.

3 Davies, R. "Keeping Faith," *Saturday Night* 102(1) January 1987, p 188.

4 Kaplan, S. and Talbot, J. "Psychological Benefits of Wilderness Experience," in Irwin Altman and Joachim F. Wohlwill, (eds.) *Behaviour and the Environment.* New York: Plenum Press, 1983, p 166.

5 Maslow, A. *Motivation and Personality.* New York: Harper, 1970.

6 Drengson, p 115.

7 Whalley, G. *The Legend of John Hornby.* Toronto: Macmillan, 1962.

8 Atwood, M. "True North," *Saturday Night* 102(1) January 1987, p 146.

9 Muir, J. in Teale, E.W. (ed.) *The Wilderness World of John Muir.* Boston: Houghton Mifflin Company, 1954, p 319.

10 Thoreau, H. in Birmingham, C. (ed.) *Winds from the Wilderness.* Toronto: Canadian Outward Bound Wilderness School, 1982, p 14.

11 Olson, S. in Birmingham, p 17.

12 Unsoeld, W. in Birmingham, p 15.

13 Trudeau, P. in Birmingham, p 16.

14 Jacques, F. in Birmingham, p 90.

15 Cayley, D. *History and the New Age*, part one,"The End of History." Transcript of IDEAS program May 10-31, 1984. Toronto: Canadian Broadcasting Corporation, 1984, p 2.

16 Bacon, S. *The Conscious Use of Metaphor in Outward Bound*. Denver: Colorado Outward Bound School, 1983.

17 Litteljohn, B. and Pearce, J. *Marked by the Wild*. Toronto: McClelland & Stewart, 1973.

18 Bacon p 58.

19 Thoreau, H.D. *A Week on the Concord and Merrimack Rivers*. New York: Bantam Books, 1962.

20 Stephenson, R., as quoted in Krutch, J.W. *Walden and Other Writings by Henry David Thoreau*. Toronto: Bantam Books, 1962, p 20.

21 James, W.C. "The Quest Pattern and the Canoe Trip" in Hodgins, B. and Hobbs, M. (eds.) *Nastawgan*. Toronto: Betelgeuse Books, 1985, p 9.

22 Litteljohn and Pearce, p 14.

23 Lopez, B. *Arctic Dreams: Imagination and Desire in a Northern Landscape*. New York: Bantam Books, p 12.

Canoeing: Towards a Landscape of the Imagination

C.E.S. Franks

The term "canoeing" needs no definition. In this title, "landscape" is the physical environment; "imagination" is the internal human context and creativity which gives meaning to that perception. In other words, what we actually perceive is a mixture of two things: *what* actually exists out there, and *how* we interpret it. The argument is that canoeing is, or at least can be, a creative act which enhances understanding of the land-scape, and that this creative act helps fulfill important human needs. The landscape of the imagination is the end product of this and other creative acts, and links the inner world with the outer world. I'm not certain where the phrase, "landscape of the imagination" comes from, but have a vague idea it originates with either Emerson or Thoreau. It was certainly something I had in mind as I wrote *The Canoe and White Water,*[12] within which I tried to place canoeing in a geographical, historical, and contemporary human context.

Cultural geographers have begun to recognize the importance of the affective and aesthetic relationships of man to the environment. One of the pioneers in studying this is the American geographer, Yi-Fu Tuan, who has written about "topophilia," or love of place:

The word "topophilia" is a neologism, useful in that it can be defined broadly to include all of the human being's affective ties with the material environment. These differ greatly in intensity, subtlety, and mode of expression. The response to the environment may be primarily aesthetic: it may then vary from the fleeting pleasure one gets from a view to the equally fleeting but far more intense sense of beauty that is suddenly revealed. The response may be tactile, a delight in the feel of air, water, earth. More permanent and less easy to express are feelings that one has toward a place because it is home, the locus of memories, and the means of gaining a livelihood.[1]

Tuan goes on to say that topophilia is not the strongest of human emotions. Love of family, for example, is much stronger. But, when topophilia is compelling, the place and environment become the carriers of emotionally-charged events, often perceived as symbols. In modern life, physical contact with the natural environment is increasingly indirect and limited to special occasions.

Technological man's involvement with nature is recreational rather than vocational. Sightseeing behind the tinted windows of a coach severs man from nature. On the other hand, in such sports as water skiing and mountain climbing, man is pitted against nature in violent contact. What people in advanced societies lack (and counter cultural groups appear to seek) is the gentle, unselfconscious involvement with the physical world that prevailed in the past when the tempo of life was slower, and that young children still enjoy.[2]

Aggressive, technical white water canoeing would not create the genuine contact with nature that Tuan advocates. For this purpose, we seek its more recreational, wilderness-based counterpart.

Many, including Tuan, argue that part of our estrangement from the landscape comes from the Christian tradition which maintained the dual and opposed meanings of wilderness: desert was both haunt of demons and realm of harmony with the creaturely world. In North America this ambiguity has been retained. On the one hand, we fear the wilderness and want to conquer it through settlement and resource extraction; on the other, we want to preserve it as our salvation. Both of these approaches deny close contact with the familiar. The fear-and-conquer approach refuses to admit any meaning other than the uses to which wilderness can be put. Idealization of it, on the other hand, willfully ignores the reality that so-called wilderness has been the homeland of native Canadians for thousands of years, and the province of non-native fur traders, among others. North Americans first feared the wilderness.[3] Then they began to love it. Now, in the affluent age of air transportation, the danger is in loving it to death.

Furthermore, some natural environments have figured prominently in humanity's dreams of the ideal world. Forest, seashore, valley, and island are all important in wilderness canoeing. The forest is an enveloping world that caters to material and spiritual needs. It was also the warm nurturing womb out of which humanity emerged. And even today the cabin in the forest clearing remains a powerful lure to the modern man who dreams of withdrawal. The sheltered cover of a shore has a twofold appeal with its geometry, on the one hand, of the recessions of beach and valley which denote security, while on the other, the open horizon to the water, which incites adventure. The valley is a diversified ecological niche that promises easy livelihood. Symbolically the valley is identified with the womb and shelter. Its concavity protects and nurtures life. The valley is feminine. The island has a tenacious hold on man's imagination. Its importance lies in this realm of the imagination. In legends the island appears as the abode of the dead or immortals. Land in watery cosmogonies appears of necessity as islands.

Another landscape that Canadian canoeists frequently meet is the Barrens, that anomalous combination of desert and water, of scarcity and richness. This landscape speaks of a nordicity which is absent from the myths and images of classical western civilization. The river, too, is important to canoeists. The river is an essential component of the valley, and river canoeing partakes of the sheltering and nurturing symbolic meaning of the valley. But the river, as white-water canoeists well know, can also be an aggressive, hostile, thrusting and linear environment. Part of the beauty of river canoeing is in this contrast between the masculine and feminine elements; these many different sorts of landscapes have different symbolic contents and meanings. These are parts of the landscape of the imagination.

The landscape of the imagination is also a place of myth. There are two meanings of myth: first, it is the unknown, an area of mystery and rumours; second, it is the spatial component of a world view, a vision and expression of localized values within which people carry on their practical day-to-day activities.

The second kind of mythical space functions as a component in a world view or cosmology. It is better articulated and more consciously held than mythical space of the first kind. World view is a people's more or less systematic attempt to make sense of environment. To be livable, nature and society must show order and display a harmonious relationship. All people require a sense of order and fitness in their environment.

Mythical space is an intellectual construct. It can be very elaborate. Mythical space is also a response of feeling and imagination to fundamental human needs.[4]

Both sorts of mythical landscapes are important to canoeists; the first, because it inspires the urge to explore, to find where the river leads, what is at the end of the portage, what lies on the other side of the watershed. This is the mythical landscape filled with equally mythical dragons, where the hardy explorer, if only in making the portage and battling mosquitoes, confronts the demons of nature and vanquishes them.

But it is the second sort of mythical landscape that is the more important—the sense of place, belonging and meaning, is fundamental to the landscape of the imagination. It is what creates the context and purpose for everyday existence, and which provides the continuity of a meaningful physical environment within and through which humanity can live, love, work, prosper, create, and die with some sense of purpose.

My argument is that we have lost our sense of place. This is the source of much of our sense of estrangement and alienation. Native Canadians had this sense of landscape and land, and this is the reason that the land, and land claims, are still so important to our native populations. This sense of landscape was not transmitted to non-native settlers in the great European invasion of North America. Instead, it was lost.

The landscape of the imagination for canoeists is too often looked at as one of great mysteries, dangers and adventure. This is not healthy. The landscape of the imagination for canoeists ought more to become one of a homeland that gives a sense of place. The continuity and context of this sort of physical and mythical reality is even more essential to humanity than adventure in the realm of the unknown.

Thomas Berger, in his enquiry into the Mackenzie Valley pipeline, distinguished north as "frontier" from north as "homeland." To non-native entrepreneurs the north is a frontier to be exploited; to the natives it was a homeland to be treasured and enjoyed. This distinction is very similar to the two kinds of landscapes: frontier is mystery and adventure; homeland is landscape of human experience.

To native Canadians, the land was very much a homeland. They were, at the time of the European invasion, dependent on the land for livelihood. Fishing, hunting, and gathering demanded an intimate understanding of the land. The land had meaning for native people that no city dweller or technological person could appreciate; and within this intimacy was their own mythology and cosmogony.

Barry Lopez, in *Arctic Dreams,* tells of his experience while camped on an island in the Arctic Ocean. Some Eskimos who were conducting a land-use survey to substantiate land claims paid Lopez's camp a visit. The two groups had a long conversation, much of it about hunting. Lopez recounts the vast volume of information about the landscape that passed back and forth:

One feels here, sharing the details of animals' lives in the memories of those present, the authority for a claim to the land just as legitimate and important as the things found at a 400-year-old-house.

After they left—they were travelling in a small boat toward the east (and to most foreign observers they would have seemed underdressed and poorly provisioned for their journey, a common impression)—we talked among ourselves about the Eskimos' cultural history. The men who left carried with them a borrowed historiography, a matrix they put down like a net in the undifferentiated sphere of time that welled up in their own traditional and unwritten history. It is a system they are becoming familiar, and handy, with. And there was great dignity and authority in the Eskimo women who sat on driftwood logs on Pingok Island, recalling into tape recorders the details of their lives from so many years ago. One could so easily imagine, as memory bloomed before the genuine desire to know, filaments appearing in the wind reattaching them to the land, even as they speak.[5]

These, and other land-use-and-occupancy studies have revealed a long and remarkably unbroken connection between various groups of indigenous people and their land.

It is impossible to separate their culture from these landscapes. The land is like a kind of knowledge travelling through time with them. Land does for them what architecture sometimes does for us. It provides a sense of place, of scale, of history.[6]

The spatial system of the Salteaux Indians of Manitoba, who live near the Berens River east of Lake Winnipeg, is similar.

The terrain they know through direct experience is essentially confined to the winter hunting and summer fishing grounds. Together these make up a small world, but one that the Salteaux Indian knows in great detail. Beyond this small world, knowledge of terrain becomes hazy and inaccurate. An Indian who works in one hunting area may be ignorant of the geography of another Indian's hunting territory. Yet all Indians will have a rough idea of the locations of the major lakes and rivers far beyond their home base, whether they have visited them or not. The small worlds of direct experience are fringed with much broader fields known indirectly through symbolic means.[7]

Most studies of Canadian natives, whether conducted for arctic pipelines, James Bay hydro development, land-claim settlements, or many other projects, have discovered that the land is an essential part of the culture.

Rootedness in the soil and the growth of pious feeling toward it seem natural to sedentary agricultural peoples. What of nomadic hunters and gatherers? Because they do not stay in one place and because their sense of land ownership is ill-defined, we might expect less attachment; but in fact the strongest sentiment for nurturing earth can exist among such people.[8]

The relationship to the land of the Indians of Northeastern British Columbia is intimate and intricate. Patterns of use for hunting and fishing are overlaid with a pattern of experience, events and history. In addition, the land forms the basis of stories, myths, and dreams. Dreams can lead to action. The Indians say that some old-timers who were great hunters found their quarry first in dreams, and later followed the trails revealed in dreams to re-encounter and kill the animals.[9] This sort of inter-relationship and harmony between the external and internal worlds, between objective experience and subconscious, between the landscape and the imagination, was an essential part of nomadic hunting life.

The Indians tried to explain their relationship with the land to the pipeline enquiry. After the formal hearing was completed, they had a feast together. The Indians brought out a dream map to show the officials. It was as large as a table top, and had been folded tightly. It was covered with thousands of markings. The Indians explained that it showed the trail to heaven, the bad places, and where the animals are. It had been discovered in dreams. But dreams get destroyed in the confrontation of cultures. The natives speak, but who is listening, or even can listen?

A Lakota woman named Elain Jahner once wrote that what lies at the heart of the religion of hunting peoples is the notion that a spiritual landscape exists within the physical landscape. To put it another way, occasionally one sees something fleeting in the land, a moment when line, colour, and movement intensify and something sacred is revealed, leading one to believe that there is another realm of reality corresponding to the physical one but different.

In the face of a rational, scientific approach to the land, which is more widely sanctioned, esoteric insights and speculations are frequently overshadowed, and what is lost is profound. The land is like poetry: it is inexplicably coherent, it is transcendent in its meaning, and it has power to elevate a consideration of human life.[10]

This is a real landscape of the imagination. Native populations had, and often still have, a strong intimacy with the land. Both the land and its mythical components are essential parts of their culture, combining to create a landscape of the imagination. This landscape of the imagination is under attack, just as native culture and traditional economy is, through the massive intrusion of non-native technological society.

The three fundamental causes for the loss of the landscape of the imagination to non-native Canadians are technology, mass culture, and ignorance. However, before going on, it is important to note that the canoe is a powerful antidote to this loss, but it is not omnipotent in this regard.

Technology can relate both to physical objects and human beings. We normally think of it exclusively in terms of the physical world—automobiles, factories, mines, television sets, chain saws—but in many ways it is the human technologies that are the more important. Human institutions and relations comprise society and hence are built into perceptions, feelings, values, attitudes, and patterns of action. They become regarded as the natural way of looking at things, as though there were no others, and this leads to a breakdown in communication, an inability to understand other cultures, and an erroneous assumption that there is only one right way (our way) to do things. These technologies impair imagination, especially when it comes to new ways of living and relating to one another and the natural world.

A. A. Milne described Winnie-the-Pooh's dilemma in this situation of being caught in one not entirely pleasant way of doing things and not being able to envisage an alternative:

Here is Edward Bear, coming downstairs now, bump, bump, bump, on the back of his head, behind Christopher Robin. It is, as far as he knows, the only way of coming downstairs, but sometimes he feels that there is really another way, if only he could stop bumping for a moment and think of it. And then he feels that perhaps there isn't.[11]

Not only modern technological societies face this problem. It is a natural part of human experience. The difference for modern technological societies is that they are so powerful, so aggressive, so expansion-oriented, that they are in danger of destroying every other alternative form of human relationship and meaning, without ever having understood what they were all about. And we, too, are not able to stop bumping long enough to think of it.

The form of human relationship and organization that is characteristic of modern technological society is the bureaucracy. The term "bureaucracy" is often used in a pejorative sense to refer to inefficient and cumbersome large-scale organizations, particularly parts of the government. But bureaucracy also has a technical, social science meaning. To a social scientist, a bureaucracy is a large-scale organization in which employment is based on professional competence and merit, in which behaviour and decisions are based on rules and rationality, and in which cases and problems are dealt with in an impersonal, objective manner. This describes the organization for which most people in the western world work: businesses, government, schools, hospitals, the military, and universities. Bureaucracies and bureaucratic norms are the common form of modern organization.

Many social scientists have examined bureaucracies, and a few have also examined the effect of bureaucratic organization on human values, relationships and vision. Perhaps the greatest of these was Max Weber, who at the end of the nineteenth century was the first to describe bureaucracies and their problems in a powerful, scholarly way. Weber said that the effect of widespread bureaucracy in society was a numbing of the human spirit, what he called a "loss of enchantment" in the modern world. The landscape no longer was a realm of myth in either of its two senses. Rather, the land and its biota and minerals became resources and raw products to be used through technology for other goals. They became simply means to economic ends for people and organizations often many thousands of miles away. The sense of place and belonging was destroyed.

Canada is surely one of the countries of the world for which this phenomenon holds most true. Our early exploration was driven by the profit-motive and carried out by large foreign businesses such as the Hudson's Bay Company; our economy has for centuries been based on the extraction and export of staple products, regardless of the effects on human beings or the landscape; our internal economy has been built upon railways and other massive achievements of transportation technology; in most of Canada, government and government bureaucracy came first, settlement later. Canada was built by, and is still held together by bureaucratic organizations, both public and private.

Correspondingly great, then, ought to be our lack of sense of place, loss of enchantment, and absence of a landscape of the imagination. We do not have a well-developed landscape of the imagination. One route which I shall not explore from this starting point is the effect of this lack on the land itself. The environmental impact of lumbering, mining, hydroelectric development, and other large-scale industries is too well known to need repeating. Canada still suffers from a hinterland treasure-chest mentality. Our political and economic rhetoric is based on massive resource extraction and conquest of wilderness. It is not one founded on a sense of the familiar and treasured homeland. Instead, I shall explore the factors—government, economics, industry, and their bureaucracies—contributing to this estrangement.

Mass culture is the first of these other contributing factors. The mass media are controlled and directed by large industrial organizations. Their interest is in profit, and the product they offer is a standardized item of general appeal to mass audiences. Since the bulk of these industries, particularly television and film, are located in the United States, the bulk of the product is situated in American locales. A television watcher anywhere in Canada is likely to be more familiar, as a result, with the landscapes of southern California than with those only a hundred miles away from home. The media, in particular television, serve to estrange Canadians from their own place, time and being. The landscape of the imagination in television is a fantasy world hundreds of miles to the south, and of a different culture.

The result is a split between the world of the imagination and the lived-in reality. The context of day-to-day living loses its familiarity and becomes part of the unknown. This makes the mythic qualities of the lived-in landscape those of the first sort, of mystery and danger, rather than what they ought to be, of the familiar and the beloved homeland. This is a unique and peculiarly modern form of alienation. It destroys the authenticity of a person's own time, place and experience.

It is not a charming comment on the understanding and attitudes of the Canadian government towards the Canadian experience that, when television was first brought to the north, the concern was to deliver southern (American) shows to remote locations. This, it was argued, would end their isolation. One result is a generation of northern natives whose perception of southern reality is Dallas and Hollywood. This has been a powerful instrument towards the destruction of native culture.

Ignorance is the third factor leading to estrangement. Both English and French culture in Canada were imported. The French have had 200 more years than the English to adapt to the Canadian context, and have done so reasonably well; the English culture in Canada is still struggling to find itself. With our primary literary sources being British and American, Canadians until recently have had very little literature which gives a sense of place and creates a mythology of the familiar within the Canadian landscape. In a very real sense we have been strangers in our own land. A Canadian voice is now beginning to be heard, but it is still not the dominant voice in popular or academic literature. The dominant voice is still foreign. It is a magnificent heritage, but it does nothing to create a Canadian landscape of the imagination.

In *The Canoe and White Water* I argued that Canadian history contains an important series of discontinuities, between native and nonnative experience, between generations, and between frontier agriculture and exploration. These discontinuities are the basis of our loss and rediscovery of white water canoeing skills. They hold true in literature, and impede the creation of a landscape of the imagination. One can read most of Pauline Johnson's poetry about canoeing and not realize that she was of Indian descent. Her paddle sang its song in imperial Victorian English, a sort of lightweight Tennyson.

Perhaps the best Canadian poet to write about canoeing was Duncan Campbell Scott. His magnificent "Rapids at Night," "Night Hymns on Lake Nipigon," "The Height of Land," and others can be appreciated as poetic visions of the experience of canoeing, but they do nothing to communicate the spirit of past generations or of native Canadians. The closest Scott comes to mentioning natives is during a storm on Lake Nipigon:

Sing we the sacred ancient hymns of churches,
Chanted first in old-world nooks of the desert,
While in the pellucid Nipigon reaches
Hunted the savage[13]

This lacuna in Scott's vision is a very important one. Scott was a senior official, and ultimately director of, the Indian Affairs Branch of the government of Canada. But nowhere in either his poetry or in his work is there any recognition on his part of the authenticity and importance of the experience and knowledge of native Canadians, nor is there the slightest suggestion that English Canadians could learn from native culture an under-standing of the landscape and the natural world. In fact, Scott saw his purpose as an administrator of Indians as one of assim-ilating ignorant, uncouth heathens. He declared his intentions to a parliamentary committee:

I want to get rid of the Indian problem. I do not think as a matter of fact, that this country ought to continuously protect a class of people who are able to stand alone. That is my whole point. Our objective is to continue until there is not a single Indian in Canada that has not been absorbed into the body politic, and there is no Indian question, and no Indian Department.[14]

Perhaps only in Canada could a man with the fine intel-lect and sensibilities of a first-class poet hold a position of administrative power over a large class of citizens and be com-pletely blind to the authenticity and value of their experience in both his poetry and his administration. Our culture is virulently imperialistic and willing to destroy weaker ones. Our un-willingness to link our heritage with that of native Canadians is strikingly illustrated by Duncan Campbell Scott, both as poet and administrator. But it neither began nor ended with him.

Natives sometimes appear in modern Canadian literature, but when they do it is as highly abstracted and idealized beings, somewhere between the natural world and ourselves, and often as the spokesmen for the natural world. Natives are not, in this literature, located in a specific landscape, but stand abstracted from it, as symbols. The real landscape of the native peoples, with its names for every natural feature and its history of hu-man deeds connected with places and names, does not survive the transition. It is lost to Canadian literature as much as it is lost to Canadian maps.

Douglas Le Pan's poem "Canoe Trip" extols the experi-ence of canoeing, but the landscape of his poem conveys no sense of the continuity of human experience. His landscape is the mythical wilderness, the land of adventure, and the place for regeneration of spirit and body:

But here are crooked norms made straight,
The fracture could no doctor call correct.
The hand and mind, reknit, stand whole for work;
The fable proves no cul-de-sac.
Now from the maze we circle back;
The map suggested a wealth of cloudy escapes.
That was a dream, we have converted the dream to act.
And what we now expect is not simplicity,
No steady breeze, or any surprise.
Orchids along the portage, white water, crimson leaves.
Content, we face again the complex task.

And yet the marvels we have seen remain.
We think of the eagles, of the fawns at the river bend,
The storms, the sudden sun, the clouds sheered downwards.
O so to move! With such immaculate decision!
O proudly as water falls curling like cumulus!

This is the standard voice used to describe the experience of canoeing in Canadian literature, though it is also often tinged, as it is in the poetry of Duncan Campbell Scott, with a sense of the potential malevolence of nature.

The landscape of the wilderness in Canadian literature is mythic in the first sense, of the adventurous, and mystical, and not in the second sense, as the friendly and familiar homeland where one's own activities share and build on the experience of generations. This, in turn, reinforces the separation of canoeing and wilderness from normal life. The separation is the sort that leads to a romantic idealization of the unknown, and a hostility towards any sort of development, even that which is compatible with wilderness experience. This mythical romanticism and divorce from the used and familiar creates a problem which bedevils park policy in Ontario as much as petroleum exploration in the Arctic. Except for native Canadians, who are few in number, there is no middle ground of a landscape of settled and continuing human experience for the Canadian north. It is a remote wilderness to canoeist, a treasure chest to be plundered by government and industry. Either vision does not include the protected and familiar homeland and sense of belonging and preserving.

In the literature on canoeing, Eric Morse's *Fur Trade Canoe Routes of Canada: Then and Now*[15] stands out as having quite a different voice. Morse, a trained historian, set out with his equally middle-aged companions to rediscover and retrace the canoe routes of the fur trade. His explorations had two dimensions: that of the historical and geographical literature, and that of the country of the canoe. His results were presented in dispassionate clear prose, and his book achieves the purposes of the historian: to make the present meaningful through understanding the past; to make the past meaningful through the experience of the present. Neither in this book nor in his posthumous memoirs[16] is the experience of wilderness canoeing coloured by romantic exaggeration of dangers and thrills.

These lines of argument lead towards identifying two different kinds of canoeing: conquering the wilderness, and enjoying a homeland. Both correspond to two different kinds of landscape of the imagination. Within limits the first can serve as a release and source of regeneration. But the second is much the preferable: it entails a living with the landscape rather than a struggling against or exploiting. The increased frequency with which Canadians travel in the wilderness might encourage the change towards the homeland sort of landscape of the imagination. So also might the increased audibility of the Indian and Inuit voice in asserting the importance and authenticity of their own experience and culture.

In opposition to these positive trends are forces which estrange us from the landscape and which look at the wilderness as a treasury to be ransacked. The real point about mass culture is that it enforces an alienation from one's own time, place and person. Our age, more than any other, is an age of mass culture. We bathe in newspapers, and drown in television.

The creation of a landscape of the imagination asserts authenticity of experience against this alienation. Canoeing is a direct, first-hand experience of the landscape at a scale and pace comparable to that of the pre-conquest native society. At lease it can be, if we listen to the voices of the past and the inhabitants of the land. For canoeing to create a landscape of the imagination, it must have a context of history, of other people's experiences, or dreams, hopes and failures. To go out and conquer the wilderness is an act of destruction whether it be through mining, hydro development, logging, or simply racing down a river oblivious to what and where it is. That is not creating an authentic landscape of the imagination; it is acting out a bad script.

An authentic landscape of the imagination is an act of rebellion against mass society. It places the individual explicitly and authentically in a context of place, time, persons, and meaning. Canoeing can be part of, and can help to create, a landscape of the imagination. Long may it do so. And long may the canoeists ensure that the rivers run. It is perhaps too much to hope that most canoeists can now learn directly from native Canadians, but they can learn indirectly. And those who venture into the wilderness should at least try to learn and, if they don't entirely succeed, they ought at least to know that they are trespassers on others' maps and dreams, and ought to recognize that they have at least the possibility of sharing, preserving, and building on a marvellous, real, familiar and, at the same time, mystical landscape of the imagination. Canada is a northern nation. A strong element of nordicity in the Canadian landscape of the imagination is essential for it to be one of our homeland. Canoeing, properly placed in its historical and cultural context, is contributing to this important component of nation-building.

Notes

1 Tuan, Y. *Space and Place: The Perspective of Experience*. Minneapolis: The University of Minnesota Press, 1977.

2 Tuan, p 96.

3 Nash, R. *Wild Rivers and the American Mind*. New Haven: Yale University Press, 1967.

4 Tuan, pp 88, 99.

5 Lopez, B. *Arctic Dreams: Imagination and Desire in a Northern Landscape*. London: Picador, 1987, p 264.

6 Lopez, p 265.

7 Hallowell, A.I. *Culture and Experience*. Philadelphia: University of Pennsylvania Press, 1955, pp 192-3. (As quoted in Tuan, pp 87-88).

8 Tuan, pp 156-7.

9 Brody, H. *Maps and Dreams: Indians and the British Columbia Frontier*. Harmondsworth: Penguin Books, 1983, pp 44-5.

10 Lopez, pp 273-4.

11 Milne, A.A. *Winnie-the-Pooh*. Toronto: McClelland and Stewart, 1925, p 3.

12 Franks, C.E.S. *The Canoe and White Water: From Essential to Leisure Sport.* Toronto: University of Toronto Press, 1977.

13 From Scott's poem "Night Hymns on Lake Nipigon."

14 Quoted in: Tilley, E. Brian. *A Narrow Vision: Duncan Campbell Scott and the Administration of Indian Affairs in Canada.* Vancouver: University of British Columbia Press, 1986, p 50.

15 Morse, Eric W. *Fur Trade Canoe Routes of Canada: Then and Now.* Toronto: University of Toronto Press, 1979.

16 Morse, Eric W. *Freshwater Saga: Memoirs of a Lifetime of Wilderness Canoeing in Canada.* Toronto: University of Toronto Press, 1987.

Back River Talking Blues

by Tom Mawhinney

As part of the opening festivities at the Canexus *conference, a minstrel wandered by and enchanted the gathering with a musical rendition of his canoeing adventures. The performer was Kingston psychologist Tom Mawhinney, and the song* Back River Talking Blues, *made a fun and fitting conference opening. The audio version of this ditty can be found on Mawhinney's latest album* Nurture the Spark *(Calliope Music, 1988). Because these lyrics, like no other contribution, capture the wonderful sense of whimsy and irreverence bred by the Canadian canoeing experience, we offer them as final words in this treatment of canoe and culture.*

If you want to get off the beaten track
Remember the voyage of Captain Back
Down the river that's his namesake
To the Arctic Circle, and Pelly Lake
It's a national historical monument, and it's popular
There's lots of loons, geese, muskox, hoary marmots,
And six hundred million mosquitoes can't be wrong.

If you never knew what intimacy meant,
It's four men sleeping in a single tent
One's snoring, another one's thrashing,
Another one's got his teeth a-gnashing ...
I'm lying awake in the corner on one elbow
Plotting my revenge
I'm gonna kick him clear across the tent before he kicks me!

In the Great Northwest, beyond the trees
You've got to learn to live without luxuries
There's no-one gargles, and no-one shaves
It takes a will of cast iron just to bathe
Water's ice cold
Atmosphere gets pretty thick
Somebody pass me that bottle of emergency spray-bomb deodorant
That man hasn't washed his armpits in three weeks!

Now, Captain George, he saw lots of sights
The conical hills, and the Northern Lights
The natural turrets, and the white stone isles
And caribou herds that stretched for miles

Pretty lively imagination
I think the Captain's been into the grog again.

Yes, the comforts are few in the Great Northwest
But of any time, mealtime's the best
The Barrens' menu's not really a treat
And you can't forget that you are what you eat:
Freeze-dried beef-flavoured soya granules
Freeze-dried chicken-flavoured soya granules
Thinkin' 'bout pizza, mille feuille, filet mignon,
And anything fresh.

If you want to know how to make a man half-crazed
You paddle your guts out for twenty-five days
Your arms are weary and your hands are sore
And you're always headed
for the farther shore
You curse the wind, and the rain, and the cold
And the very thought of adventures bold
What's that? Somebody wants to know when
you're going up there again?
Not too soon, really ...
Be glad to help you plan your next trip, though!

Contributors

EDITORS

James Raffan, editor of books including *Wild Waters: Canoeing Canada's Wilderness Rivers*, was the *Canexus* conference program coordinator. He is a well-travelled adventurer and productive writer who teaches at Queen's University Faculty of Education.

Bert Horwood is the author of a number of books, the most recent of which is *Experiential Education in High School: Life in the Walkabout Program.* He has special commitment to learning from the natural and cultural environments. He currently teaches at Queen's University Faculty of Education where his research includes exploration of learning on high school canoe trips.

CONTRIBUTORS

E.Y. Arima is an ethnohistorian with National Historic Parks and Sites, Environment Canada—Parks. He has a special interest in native watercraft, and generally in the context-conscious study of material culture in anthropology.

Philip Chester is a talented poet, teacher, and the creative force behind the Ottawa Valley outfitting company *Blazing Paddles.* In his long study of Canadian wilderness literature, he has developed a passion for Grey Owl's life and writing. He lives in Deep River, Ontario.

C.E.S. Franks is the author of several books including *The Canoe and White Water.* He is an avid wilderness paddler, and lives in Kingston, Ontario where he teaches in the Political Studies Department of Queen's University.

Shelagh Grant has travelled in and written extensively about northern Canada. She was a contributor to *Nastawgan* and is the author of an upcoming UBC Press book entitled *Sovereignty or Security: Government Policy in the Canadian North.* She teaches Canadian History at Trent University.

Bob Henderson combines his interests in Canadian Studies and outdoor travel in his work at McMaster University. There he is well known for toting a lunch of fire-browned bannock. His prolific writing includes regular contributions to *Explore* and *Paddler* magazines, and a chapter about Saskatchewan's Clearwater River in *Wild Waters.*

Bruce Hodgins, co-editor of *Nastawgan*, is Director of Camp Wanapitei in Temagami, and is an avid paddler and historian who has written extensively about the north. He teaches at Trent University and is Director of its graduate program in Canadian Heritage and Development Studies.

Gwyneth Hoyle is a writer and the librarian at Peter Robinson College at Trent University, currently studying Canadian history, region by region. Her article"Women of Determination: Northern Journeys by Women Before 1940" was published in *Nastawgan*.

William C. James teaches in the Queen's University Department of Religion, and is the author of the seminal article "The Canoe Trip as a Religious Quest," first published in *Studies in Religion*. His other writings include two recent books: *A Fur Trader's Photographs* and *Needle to the North*.

C. Fred Johnston was one of the prime movers behind the *Canexus* conference. His interest in canoeing history has led to a number of articles including the "Canadian Canoe" entry in the *Canadian Encyclopedia*. He teaches Educational Technology at Queen's University Faculty of Education.

George J. Luste started canoeing with a solo trip to Moosonee in 1962, and since then has paddled or snowshoed in nearly every major watershed in the country. He was a contributor to *Nastawgan*, and teaches in the Physics Department at the University of Toronto.

Roderick A. Macdonald is a paddler and a prolific writer on legal matters. He lives in Montreal where he is Dean of Law at McGill University.

Kenneth G. Roberts, former assistant editor for *Saturday Night*, has been a writer and paddler for many years. His best known work is *The Canoe*, co-written with Philip Shackleton.

Kirk A.W. Wipper has a consuming passion for canoes and canoeing that led him to found the Kanawa International Museum, associating his name with canoeing globally. Since retiring from the University of Toronto in 1985, he has become National Director of the Duke of Edinburgh Award Program.

ILLUSTRATOR

Bill Mason is Canada's best known paddler because of his famous films and best-selling book *Path of the Paddle*. He completed his film-making career recently to devote all of his time to writing, painting, playing hockey, and illustrating books that match his passion.

Q

Quebec   169
Quebec paddle industry   110
Quetico Provincial Park   84
Quixote, Don   34, 96
    Rozinante   96

R

rafting   97
Rasmussen, Knud   157, 158
Rat River   18
RCMP   6
Reid, Bill   81
Renaissance   131
Rice Lake   64, 66, 139
Richards, George   139
Riel, Louis   96
river   125
    as hostile environment   189
    as place of beauty   189
    as teacher   125
river-bagger   84
Roberts, Kenneth   6, 7, 28, 75, 95
Rohmer, Richard   14
Roosevelt, Theodore   15, 136
Roth, Philip   34
Rousseau   128
rowing   62
Royal Canoe Club   61
Russell, Frank   16

S

Saturday Night Live   93
Savannah Portage   119
Schwatka, Frederick   114
Scott, Duncan Campbell   197, 198
Seal Lake   141
Service, Robert   17
Seton, Ernest Thompson   18
Shackleton, Philip   6, 7, 28, 75

Simpson, Sir George   50
Smoke Lake   84
Snoopy (cartoon)   132
Spence, John D.   20
Stanton, Leigh   139
Starkell, Dana   33
Starkell, Don   33-34
Stefansson, Vilhjalmur   14
Stephenson, John   64
Stephenson, Robert Louis   182
Stoney Lake   15, 67
Strickland, Samuel   64
St. Lawrence River   15, 147
Suchman, Nancy   40
Sullivan, Rosemary   30
superheroes   94
Supreme Court of Canada   168-169
Susan River   136
symbolism   10, 189

T

Tate brothers   81
Tennyson, Alfred Lord   197
Thames River   61
Thelon River   97, 178
Thompson, David   50
Thompson, Tom   19
Thoreau, Henry David   14, 89, 179, 182, 187
Toronto Canoe Club   67, 68
tracking   113
Trekkers Outing Club   124, 127, 130, 131
trickster   131, 132
Tuan, Yi-Fu   152, 157, 187, 189
Turner, Victor   36
Tyrrell, Edith   155
Tyrrell, J.B.   52, 154, 155
Tyson, Robert   67

U

umiak   9, 38
Ungava Bay   135, 140
Unger, Jim   129, 132
U.S. Constitution   165